The Crafter's Guide to
PATTERNS

A RotoVision book

Published in 2015 by Search Press Ltd.
Wellwood, North Farm Road
Tunbridge Wells
Kent, TN2 3DR

This book is produced by
RotoVision SA, Sheridan House, 114 Western Road
Hove, BN3 1DD

ISBN 978-1-78221-219-5

Publisher: Mark Searle
Editorial Director: Isheeta Mustafi
Editor: Erin Chamberlain
Assistant Editor: Tamsin Richardson
Art Director: Lucy Smith
Layout: Suzie Johanson and Michelle Rowlandson
Cover Design: Michelle Rowlandson
Photography: Jessica Nichols

The Crafter's Guide to
PATTERNS

Create your own hand-printed designs

JESSICA SWIFT

SEARCH PRESS

CONTENTS

This page: Screen printed fabric by Jessica Swift. Photo by Jessica Nichols (**left**). Paloma bookends by Wolfum. Photo by Dan Rider, J6 Creative (**right**). **Opposite:** Screen printed apron, screen printed and embroidered pillow and Octopurse Frolic clutch by Sarah Watts for Peking Handicraft. Photo by Scott Cormack (**left**). Screen printed Bowls fabric in Graphite, Persimmon and Lemon Slice colourways by Skinny laMinx. Photo by Heather Moore (**right**).

FABRIC, P. 72

GIFT WRAP, P. 84, AND STATIONERY, P. 96

PACKAGING, P. 108

IN THE HOME, P. 120

INTRODUCTION

I've always been drawn to the decorative arts, to things that are beautiful for beauty's sake. What would our world be without beautiful artwork and patterns to fill it? It's hard to even imagine!

Patterns are everywhere – in our homes, on our clothes, on the packaging and products we buy, in the natural world. They're prolific in the world today (and have been for millennia) because they are a wonderful, simple way to infuse an endless variety of surfaces with colour, happiness, texture, charm and beauty.

Making colourful objects is deeply ingrained in me, and has been from my childhood. When I found design blogs in my twenties, I discovered artists called surface pattern designers who created the most beautiful patterns and products I'd ever seen. I glimpsed my future! I immediately began trying to learn how to create patterns, which led to my love of hand-printing. I carved stamps and attempted to print my own wallpaper, I hand-printed napkins, I used my stamps in paintings, I gradually taught myself how to use digital illustration programs. I loved creating patterns so much in those early days, and today my passion for pattern and hand-printing still runs deep and strong.

If you have a love for pattern design and are looking for a way to dive in to this world like I was, this book is for you.

In Section One, you'll learn some pattern design basics: different types of patterns, layouts and how they each work. You'll learn to create each type of pattern on paper and then how to digitise them. You'll then learn how to use your patterns to print by hand using a variety of different techniques.

In Section Two, you'll take these techniques and apply them to printing on actual surfaces. None of the projects need special equipment or expensive, fancy supplies. A trip to the art shop and a look around your house or studio will yield all the supplies necessary to begin creating your own hand-printed patterns.

The projects in each chapter of Section Two are designed to serve as jumping off points for your own experimentation with the different techniques and types of patterns shown in the book. You can create whichever type of repeating pattern you like using any of the hand-printing techniques from Section One - everything in this book is interchangeable.

There are no rules in my pattern-filled world!

Jessica Swift

Fabric by Monaluna. Photo by Jennifer Moore **(top left)**. Hand-printed gift wrap by Jessica Swift. Photo by Jessica Nichols **(top right)**. Decorative matchboxes by BelloPop. Photo by Andreina Bello **(bottom left)**. Bowls fabric and cushions in Lemon Slice, Persimmon and Graphite colourways by Skinny laMinx. Photo by Heather Moore **(bottom right)**.

Abbreviation used in this book
(o) = optional throughout

PROJECT INDEX

Inside this book you'll find a variety of do-it-yourself projects, ranging from relatively simple, once you have the techniques under your belt, to a bit more complex. They will show you how to make all sorts of surfaces sing with patterned beauty!

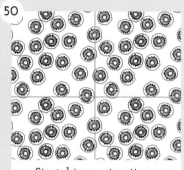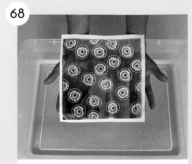

76

Screen printing a Furoshiki

78

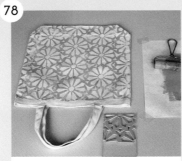

Foam stamping a tote bag

88

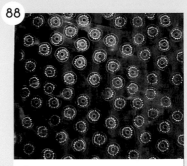

Cyanotype printing on paper

90

Foam stamping gift wrap

100

Stamping cards and envelopes

102

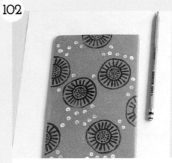

Printing on a notebook

112

Potato stamping a box

114

Stencilling a paper bag

124

Stencilling a border on a wall

126

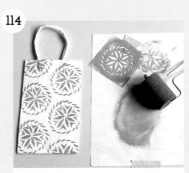

Printing on tiles

AN OVERVIEW OF PATTERN DESIGN

Have you ever wondered when and why people started adorning objects and surfaces with repeating motifs? Or where in the world the first pattern was ever created? This question is impossible to answer, but what we do know is this . . .

Decorative patterns are practically as old as time itself.

That may be a slight exaggeration, but cultures throughout the world have created patterns for centuries and used them to adorn and decorate important buildings, homes, clothing, fabric, everyday objects, ceremonial objects, and more. Remnants of woven patterned fabric have been found in Africa that date back to the ninth century BCE. Isn't that incredible?

There are many different ways to create patterns, some more complicated than others. Designers' lives are often easier today than in decades past thanks to computer programs. It's not always as necessary as it once was to design on paper with mathematical precision, as everything can now be edited, moved and manipulated on a computer. But designing patterns by hand on paper is a beautiful and useful skill to develop and will aid in any computer pattern work you may do.

Despite computers, creating successful repeat patterns can still require a good deal of thought and planning. The amount depends simply on the type of design you intend to create and the level of complexity. Whether you use a computer in your work or not, understanding the structure beneath different types of pattern is vital. Without a knowledge of the basic building blocks, designing a unique pattern will be a challenge.

As you read on, you'll learn about the important concept of the pattern tile. It is the foundation of every single pattern that exists in the world. Once you learn and understand how patterns are constructed, I'm willing to bet that you'll try to deconstruct every pattern you see in the world from now on. Just wait and see!

Pattern design is an incredibly versatile field and it's enjoying a major resurgence. Coupled with the masses of opportunities offered by the Internet to create, manufacture and sell products, there is a wide variety of beautiful patterned products available to us today. Sometimes I wonder: How will future generations refer to this current crafty and pattern-filled era in which we live, and where will our place among famous art movements like Art Nouveau, mid-century Modern and Arts and Crafts be? Only time will tell.

Now it's time to jump in and get our hands dirty! Are you ready?

Smartphone case pattern designed by Jessica Swift for Case-Mate Viorina. Photo by Jessica Swift.

Section One

PLANNING PATTERNS

Chapter One

SOURCING INSPIRATION

A common misconception about inspiration is that you have to wait for it to strike. You're probably familiar with the idea of inspiration flashing into your mind like a lightning bolt, causing a frenzy of creative activity and energy. You're at the mercy of the inspiration gods - when they decide it's a good day to visit, creativity flows and you create effortlessly. On the days they don't visit, you sit and wait, hoping they'll come back tomorrow. You can't create without inspiration. Or can you?

I don't believe that inspiration strikes from somewhere outside of you. I believe inspiration lives inside of you and that you cause it to show up. The simple act of putting that first brushstroke onto a canvas, or that first black line onto paper, or putting your camera to your eye and walking outside, causes inspiration to bubble up from within you and out through your hands and heart. Simply showing up and starting to work, even if you don't feel inspired, is one of the most important parts of finding inspiration in your pattern making.

A full creative well will provide you with inspiration from which to draw when you sit down to create. You can't find inspiration within yourself if your well is empty and dried up. Saturating your senses and getting out in the world will keep your mind and body vibrating with ideas that will show up when you begin creating your patterns. Inspiration is all around you if you're willing to look for it. Fill your creative well with colours, shapes, textures, experiences, questions, objects you love and whatever else feeds your soul.

Getting out in nature is one of the best ways to start. It's one of the world's greatest muses, with its abundance of shapes, colours, textures, patterns and beauty. Simply walking through your neighbourhood or a park and keeping your eyes open to what's around you will yield wonderful inspiration. Take a sketchbook with you and draw interesting shapes, pretty flowers, patterns you notice.

Travel, magazines, books, vintage fabrics, old photographs, museums, gift stores and billboards are all great ways to fill your senses and invite inspiration. Keep your eyes open and curious for things that delight you wherever you go.

All photos opposite by Jessica Swift.

BUILDING MOOD BOARDS

A mood board is a collection of images, colours, textures, feelings and ideas that is used as a visual tool for organising and conveying an idea. It can be physical or digital, large or small, finely detailed or loosely organised.

Mood boards are a wonderful way to distil your inspiration into a defining theme or concept for your patterns and to help you clarify what you want to create. Because they are visual documents, they serve to help you imagine what you're aiming to create, to give you a starting point and direction in which to move. Mood boards can be centred around a variety of different themes, such as colour, subject, texture, shape, culture, style, era, feeling or motif.

COLLAGE MOOD BOARDS

Creating a collage mood board is simple and fun. All you need is a large sheet of card or thick

paper, a glue stick, scissors and a variety of paper (such as stacks of magazines, paint swatches, photographs, old greeting cards and scrapbook paper). Cut out everything that catches your eye. Don't think too much about it. Once you've finished cutting out images, look at what you've gathered and see if you notice any themes. Maybe you've got a lot of blue images, or a lot of flowers. Perhaps your images all feel romantic, or edgy or happy. Start grouping images together and see if a theme begins to develop. Once you've chosen your theme, go back and cut more images to support that theme. When your collection of images feels complete, glue them onto your card. Your board can be haphazard and organic, or neat and geometric - there are no rules here. Alternatively, you can choose your theme in the beginning and find images to support that theme from the outset.

DIGITAL MOOD BOARDS

Creating mood boards on a computer is quite straightforward using design programs. You can scan images for use in your mood boards, or you can search for inspiring images online to include in your boards.

Some popular websites, such as Pinterest and Polyvore have taken mood boards to a whole new level and make it easy to collect inspiring images and hold them all in one place. Adding to and subtracting from your mood board is quick and easy, so you can change and refine your boards whenever you like.

SOURCING IDEAS FOR PATTERNS

When looking for ideas for patterns, keep your sketchbook close by. Use it as a place to store ideas for shapes, colour palettes, themes, and so on. Your sketchbook is a container, your own personal library of ideas and a wealth of inspiration – take it with you wherever you go and fill it up with visual information and reminders.

It's helpful to keep a running list of ideas for patterns. That way, if you feel uninspired, your list will be a great starting point. Brainstorm things you might like to draw. Flowers, robots, aeroplanes, mandalas, cats, maps, houndstooth, arrows, palm trees, diamonds, birds . . . your options are limitless. Ideas for patterns can come from all sorts of places, depending on what your interests are. The natural world, bookshops, libraries, objects in your home, your pets, movies, fashion runways, fabric shops, travel photos, gardens, museums, aquariums and department stores are just a few great places to start looking.

Books are great places to find ideas for patterns. I love books that catalogue objects like flowers and plant shapes, types of birds and designs from different countries around the world. Royalty-free clip art books and websites are great resources for artists. Royalty-free (also called public domain)

means the images are not held under any copyright. Books such as these are very useful as inspiration for your creative work. Although the images are available for public use, I don't advise directly copying or incorporating these types of images into your designs without any changes.

Fabric shops are also great places for inspiration. A fun way to create unique patterns is to put a creative spin on classic pattern types like paisley, houndstooth, chinoiserie or damask. How can you take a classic and make it all your own?

Discovering different pattern design eras can also infuse some fresh energy into your own patterns. Try an Internet search for Art Deco, Art Nouveau or mid-century Modern patterns and see what you find? It's fascinating to see the way different artists have approached similar subject matter like flowers and stripes over the decades.

A few books that Jessica uses, along with a peek at her sketchbook. Photo by Jessica Swift.

LEGAL CONSIDERATIONS

While it's wonderful to find inspiration in the work of others,
please take care not to directly copy any ideas, shapes, motifs
or colourways that you find in books, fabric shops, on the Internet
or elsewhere. Make sure you use these resources only
as jumping off points for your own creativity.

Copying someone else's work or using elements of someone's designs in your own work is a copyright violation and can lead to sticky situations and even lawsuits. It's easy these days to find images online, and it's important to understand that just because an image is on the Internet, it does not mean it's free to use in your own work in any form. It's best to avoid these types of situations altogether and develop your own style and way of creating and using images.

Royalty-free (or public domain) images are not held under any copyright and are available for public use without danger of copyright violation. An Internet search for 'royalty-free clip art' yields many results with hundreds of thousands of available images, and you can often purchase one image at a time, or sheets of several images. Books of royalty-free clip art images are readily available in the art section in bookshops and at online book retailers. I don't recommend using these images in your work without any digital manipulation, but legally it is fine to do so.

WHAT ABOUT VINTAGE IMAGES?

Vintage designs are generally in the public domain. The term 'vintage' means any design created before 1923. Copyright protection for

ROYALTY-FREE RESOURCES
Publications
www.doverpublications.com
www.schifferbooks.com

Websites
store.doverpublications.com
www.doverpictura.com
www.pdclipart.org
www.clipart.com
www.wpclipart.com

images created between 1923 and 1995 vary, and copyright protection for images created after 1995 lasts for the life of the artist plus 70 years. For more detailed information on copyright laws, visit your country's government copyright website.

Sometimes artists use vintage designs as starting points for their own designs. If you plan to go down this route, please make sure you are absolutely certain the designs you're using are copyright-free.

Screen printed Brancusi Stripe and Rough Diamond fabric in Inkspot colourway by Skinny laMinx. Photo by Heather Moore.

Chapter Two

COLOUR

Ever since I was a little girl, I've loved colour. Some of my favourite days as a child were shopping for bits and bobs for school, because it meant I got a new set of coloured markers. I remember happily plonking myself down on the floor, armed with my new markers and a giant sheet of paper, busily creating bubble letter posters for birthdays, holidays and for all imaginable celebrations. I carefully filled each letter with a different, colourful hand-drawn pattern and I remember the feeling of delight and satisfaction that washed over me each time I discovered a new and unusual way to combine colours. That delight is still with me today. It now comes from smearing paint on a canvas, block printing shapes upon colourful shapes and watching patterns come alive on my computer screen, but the original seed of discovery and satisfaction is still the same.

For some, colour may seem intimidating. Perhaps you've seen a colour wheel and thought that in order to use colour 'the right way' you need to know a lot about colour theory. While it is true that it is useful to know some colour theory, I'm going to suggest something radical here:

You don't need to know a thing about colour theory in order to use colour beautifully. There is no right or wrong way to use colour.

Colour is all about play. It's about trusting your intuition and your own two eyes. It's about exploring which colour palettes feel right. Think about the types of colour combinations that you love and the kinds you dislike. For example, my favourite colours together are orange and green. Any shade of orange paired with any shade of green. I use variations of this colour combination in my own work all the time. On the other hand, I'm not a fan of bright red, bright yellow and bright blue (the primary colours) together, so I never use them together in my work.

What colour combinations do you gravitate towards, and which do you stay away from? Being aware of your answers to these questions is a great place to start when you begin deciding which colours to use in your own patterns. As you experiment with different colours together, you'll discover the ways you intuitively like to combine them.

Wellington boots by Jessica Swift. Photo by Deana Levine.

CHOOSING COLOURS

While there is no right or wrong way to use colour, you can learn
a few tips and tricks to help make your colour palette sing.

2. USE ANALOGOUS COLOURS TOGETHER

Analogous colours are adjacent on the colour wheel. For example: yellow, green and blue. They look lovely together and are often found in nature. Using colour in this way will give your patterns instant harmony. To add dynamic energy to your work, add in a complementary colour, too.

1. USE COMPLEMENTARY COLOURS TOGETHER

Complementary colours are across from one another on the colour wheel. They contrast each other nicely, but can appear a bit overwhelming when used together in competing bright, vibrant hues. Try using different shades and tints of the two colours together to find visually interesting combinations. For example: rust red and lime green; tangerine orange and denim blue; or yellow ochre and lavender. When the values of both colours are bright and vibrant, it's best to use one as the main colour and one as an accent.

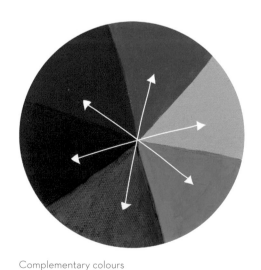

The colour wheel can help you visualise the way colours work together and how they are related to one another. If you're stuck for colour inspiration, start with the colour wheel.

Complementary colours

4. NEUTRALS + BRIGHTS = YES!

Using neutral colours will ensure that your bright colours are the centre of attention - neutral colours tend to recede into the background. Neutrals can also help ground your design and keep it from getting overwhelming. They are colours like grey, brown, white, black, khaki, navy and beige.

3. USE LIGHT AND DARK COLOURS TOGETHER

It's a good idea to vary the values of colours within your designs. When all the colour values (relative lightness or darkness) are the same, the colours compete for your eyes' attention and can appear overwhelming, harsh or muddy. Your patterns will feel more dynamic and exciting with a wide range of colour values. An obvious choice for light and dark colours is black and white, but what about interesting combinations like maroon and mint green? Or sky blue and navy blue? Or lemon yellow and dark brown?

5. LOOK AT THE WORLD AROUND YOU AND NOTICE COLOUR

Start seeing the colour all around you and you'll intuitively know which colours to choose.

BUILDING A COLOUR PALETTE

Your colour palette can include as many or as few colours as you'd like.
I often work with six to eight colours, but your palette can just as
easily consist of two colours or 24. There is no limit here!

If you're not sure where to begin, colour websites such as www.colourlovers.com and www.design-seeds.com are fantastic places for inspiration. Books and magazines are also great places to go digging for interesting colour palette ideas. Here are a few techniques to help you begin building beautiful colour palettes.

PULL YOUR COLOUR PALETTE FROM A PHOTOGRAPH OR IMAGE

Decide how many colours you'd like your palette to include. Now choose colours directly from your inspiration photograph. Instant colour palette!

USE PAINT SWATCHES TO MIX AND MATCH COLOURS

Pay a visit to your local paint or hardware store to gather some paint swatches. Cut them into squares and use them to mix and match different colour palettes. This is a wonderful way to mix and match colours that you might have never paired together. It might be useful to try the previous technique with this method as well and begin with just two colours, adding one new colour at a time. Once you've built your complete palette, experiment with switching out one of the colours to see how that changes your palette's look and feel.

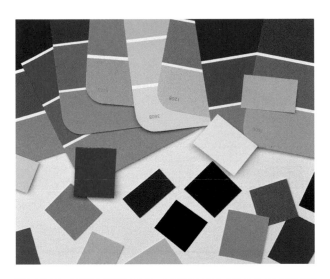

BEGIN WITH YOUR MAIN COLOUR PAIRING AND BUILD FROM THERE

Another way to begin is to decide how many colours you'd like to work with in your palette. For example, perhaps you'll choose to work with six colours. Next, decide what your main colour pairing will be. Perhaps orange and green. Play with this pairing until you find two hues that you like together. Add new colours by experimenting with how one colour at a time looks and feels with your initial orange and green pairing. Perhaps a light pink would look nice? Or a poppy red? Experiment with one colour at a time, to see how it adds to the whole, until you work up to your desired number of colours.

Chapter Three

PATTERN AND LAYOUT TYPES

If you've ever looked at a repeating pattern and wondered how in the world you would create something like that, you are not alone! Patterns can seem puzzling and complicated until you discover the magical key to unlocking the mystery of how they are put together. In pattern design, motifs, that is, the elements within a pattern, are arranged into a repeating design in a variety of ways: the straight repeat, half-drop repeat and brick repeat. At the base of each repeat style is a core rectangle or square, often called the pattern tile. The pattern tile is the foundation for the entire repeating pattern. Patterns and how they were created were completely baffling to me until I understood that every pattern is built upon a simple rectangle. I'll never forget the day that I finally learned how to successfully create a pattern tile – my life has not been the same since!

The trick to creating a visually interesting and successful pattern lies within this all-important pattern tile. To mask the underlying rectangular grid, some of the motifs in a pattern are often placed to overlap the edges of the rectangle. The key to creating a pattern tile that repeats seamlessly is to make sure the elements that overlap the edge are picked back up in exact alignment on the opposite side. Depending on the type of repeat you're creating, the exact placement on the opposite side of the rectangle varies.

You can create pattern tiles by hand or on a computer, using design and image editing programs. We will focus on creating repeats by hand, though there is some instruction on the basics of how to turn your hand-drawn patterns into digital patterns using Adobe Photoshop and Adobe Illustrator. When designing patterns, thinking through how they will look when complete is vital. How large or small will the motifs be? In what direction will the pattern best be viewed? How will you lay out and space your motifs? There are some basic principles and ideas to keep in mind as you begin to create your own patterns to achieve the best look possible.

Meadow Fabric Collection by Leah Duncan. Photo by Art Gallery Fabrics.

MOTIF STYLES

Motifs are, quite simply, the visual elements of a pattern. It is impossible to count the many different types of motifs – just take a walk down an aisle of a fabric shop and you'll probably see patterns ranging from diamonds to plaids to cityscapes to strawberries to kittens to polka dots! They can, however, generally be arranged into three broad categories: geometrics, florals and novelty. These categories are fairly broad themselves, but they serve as a useful way to group different types of patterns together. Within each category exist smaller sub-categories, some of which are listed.

GEOMETRIC

A geometric pattern, or geometric print, is one composed of non-representational shapes like squares, circles, lines, triangles, diamonds or dots. The motifs determine whether a pattern falls into this category, not the layout type. For example, a pattern made of diamond-shaped motifs can be arranged in either a structured or a tossed layout and both are considered geometric repeats. These types of patterns can be complex and intricate, simple and basic, bold and whimsical. Geometric prints are decorative useful, and are plentiful in the design world. Motifs like stripes, plaids, hounds-tooth, checks and polka dots all fall into the geometric category.

FLORAL

Floral motifs are mainly composed of flowers. These types of patterns can also incorporate motifs related to flowers (such as leaves and branches), but the most important or prolific elements in the pattern are flower shapes.

Floral motifs can be stylised, representational, symmetrical or organic, and they can be laid out in tossed or set repeats. No matter what the flowers look like, if they're a focal point of your pattern, you've created a floral print. Artists and designers have been creating floral motifs for centuries. This is a well-loved category.

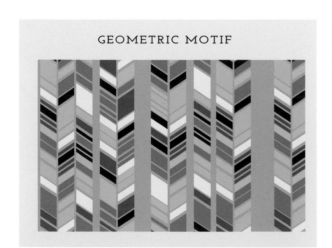

GEOMETRIC MOTIF

FLORAL MOTIF

NOVELTY (ALSO CONVERSATIONAL OR OBJECT PRINTS)

Novelty motifs are the broadest category of all. Quite simply, everything that is not a geometric print or a floral print is a novelty print. Motifs in novelty prints tend to be recognisable and representational shapes.

Objects such as fruit, robots, animals, alphabets, cars and trucks, kitchen items, space, feathers, princesses, sunglasses and bikes all fall into the category of novelty prints. While they are often fun and whimsical, the audience for any given novelty print is often smaller than for a more decorative geometric or floral pattern, since the motifs are more personal. For example, the audience for robot patterns generally tends to be young children (mostly boys), and the audience for a dog pattern might be limited to dog lovers.

COMBINING DIFFERENT TYPES OF MOTIFS

What do you do when you want to combine flowers with kittens, stripes with trees, or robots with squares? Is that allowed?

Of course it's allowed! In fact, I think crossing over between categories can make for some fun, interesting and fresh types of patterns. A pattern crosses over into a different category as soon as you introduce a motif that falls into that category into the design. For example, adding a vibrant flower to your geometric design automatically takes your pattern into the floral category, even if the geometric piece is a strong portion of the design. If you added a bike motif into a stripe pattern, your design becomes a novelty print. Take the bike out, and you're back to a geometric design.

There are no rules here. Play around and see what kinds of cool patterns you can create using all different types of motifs.

NOVELTY MOTIFS

BACKGROUNDS AND BORDERS

Backgrounds and borders are a fun way to add some depth, dimension and variety to your designs. Experimenting with different textures, shapes and colours in the background and along the edges of your designs can yield some fun and unexpected pattern play!

BACKGROUNDS

The background (also called the ground) of a pattern is the part that appears farthest away from the viewer. You do not have to limit yourself to working on solid-coloured backgrounds in your patterns. Backgrounds can also be comprised of textures, other patterns or any type of shape. It's common for backgrounds to contain small or subtle geometric motifs such as stripes, dots or plaids, but you can use other objects in the background as well, such as flowers, leaves or line work.

A strong background technique is to copy the shapes of your motifs, fill them with a solid colour that is a bit darker or lighter than the background colour and layer those shapes right on top of the background. This technique creates depth and visual interest without distracting from the main motif.

Backgrounds are generally non-directional (meaning the pattern looks the same when viewed from all angles) or two-directional (the pattern will look the same when viewed from the top or the bottom), and they are generally more subtle than the main motifs. If the background is too strong and competes with the foreground and main design motifs, it can be jarring to the eye and the pattern will not look balanced.

NON-DIRECTIONAL BACKGROUND

TWO-DIRECTIONAL BACKGROUND

PLANNING PATTERNS

BORDERS

Border designs are created when the main motif runs along the bottom or top edge (or both edges) of a pattern tile, with either a solid colour or a simple motif filling the rest of the design. They can be created by hand or on a computer. These types of patterns are often created with specific end-uses in mind, like clothing, tablecloths, tote bags and wallpaper border trim. For these types of applications, border designs are created using a straight repeat technique, creating long, repetitive borders. You can create your own simple border designs by repeating one motif across a long area, like the bottom of a piece of fabric, the bottom of a skirt or along the top of a wall in your home, creating one long, patterned stripe.

Hand-printed tiles by Jessica Swift (see p. 126 for tutorial). Photo by Jessica Nichols.

DIFFERENT BORDER ARRANGEMENTS

PATTERN TYPES

Let's dive into the more technical aspects of pattern design and look at the three main ways to construct a repeating pattern. Pay close attention, we're talking about the mysterious pattern tile now, step one on your road to understanding how patterns work!

STRAIGHT REPEAT (ALSO BLOCK REPEAT OR SQUARE REPEAT)

A straight repeat is the most basic type of repeating pattern. The motifs are arranged to either remain within a core rectangle or to overlap it and then repeat in a simple grid formation, up and down, and side to side. The motifs within the core rectangle can be simple or complicated, arranged randomly (to mask the underlying grid formation) or uniformly (making the underlying grid more noticeable). Despite slight changes in your layout, the pattern repeats the same way.

HALF-DROP REPEAT

A half-drop repeat is based on a core rectangle which repeats up and down, but instead of repeating side to side, alternating columns of the design drop half-way down the height of the pattern tile, creating a fluid, diagonal motion with the repeat. Half-drops help make the core rectangle in a repeat less obvious, because it breaks up any lines that would be created if motifs were arranged in a straight grid-like formation. You can also create repeats using a quarter drop, three-quarter drop, and so on.

STRAIGHT REPEAT

HALF-DROP REPEAT

BRICK REPEAT

A brick repeat is similar to a half-drop repeat, but instead of alternating columns dropping down half the height of the pattern tile, alternating rows shift halfway across the width of the pattern tile, to create a brick-like formation.

Like half-drop repeats, brick repeats also help to break up any unintentional lines that can be formed by repeating motifs in a grid-like fashion, making the motif less obvious and blocky and adding movement and visual interest to a design.

As with half-drop repeats, the rows in your design do not necessarily have to shift half a step; you can also create a brick repeat with a quarter shift, three-quarter shift or any other measurement you'd like.

Brick repeats are often used in clamshell layouts and medallion repeats (see pp. 38–39).

BRICK REPEAT

Fabric design and photo by Susanne Firmenich (Hamburger Liebe). Photo by Susanne Firmenich.

LAYOUT TYPES

Motifs within a pattern can be laid out in many different
ways and can be adapted to be used in the straight, half-drop
or brick repeat patterns. Motifs can be arranged to look as if they're
tossed randomly or they can be arranged in a more structured fashion
(called a set layout), in which repetition is an important feature
in the design. Neither option is inherently a better choice than
the other; the type of layout you choose depends ultimately
on your goals for your finished pattern.

TOSSED REPEAT (OR RANDOM REPEAT)

In a tossed repeat the motifs of a pattern are
scattered throughout the design, and the repeat
in this type of design is not obvious or easy to pick
out, even if it's built as a straight repeat. It should
be difficult for a viewer to figure out where the
pattern tile is and how the design repeats.

DIAMOND REPEAT

A commonly used type of set layout is a diamond
repeat. This type of layout is essentially a grid of
squares or rectangles, rotated 45° to create a grid
of diamonds. Motifs are contained within the
diamond-shaped grid, creating a lovely diagonal
motif formation.

TOSSED REPEAT

DIAMOND REPEAT

OGEE REPEAT

An ogee repeat is similar to a diamond repeat, but the sides of the diamond are smoothed out and rounded, to make a striking onion-shaped motif that repeats beautifully.

HEXAGON REPEAT

A hexagon repeat, which resembles a beehive repeat, is not as common as a diamond or an ogee repeat, but it's a fun type of set layout to experiment with.

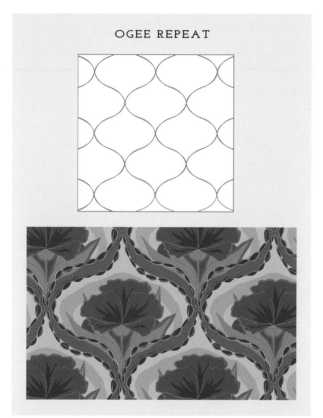

OGEE REPEAT

HEXAGON REPEAT

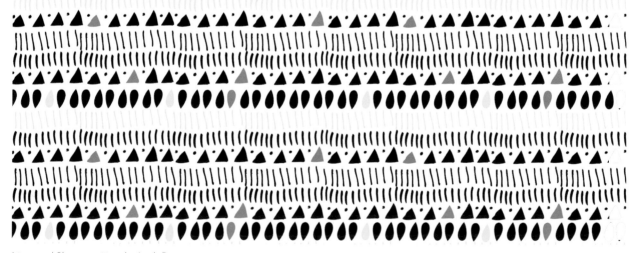

Lines and Shapes pattern by Leah Duncan.

MEDALLION REPEAT

This type of set repeat is like a hexagonal repeat except that all the edges are smoothed out to form circles. Medallion repeats often involve bold colours and are intricately detailed.

STRIPES

Stripes are a classic way to lay out a design. They can be simple or complicated, and are formed using long lines of colour or strings of motifs in varying widths. The stripes can be straight, wavy or zigzagged.

MEDALLION REPEAT

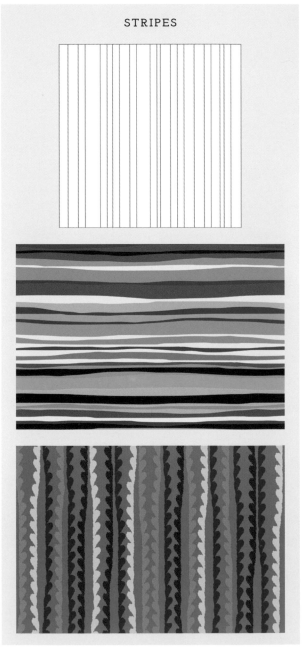

STRIPES

PLANNING PATTERNS

TESSELLATIONS

Tessellations are set layouts that are built on a foundation of interlacing and interlocking geometric shapes without any gaps or overlaps. This type of repeat is common in Islamic and Middle Eastern art and is a fascinating type of layout with which to experiment.

CLAMSHELL REPEAT (OR SCALE REPEAT)

This well-loved and common set layout type uses overlapping arcs or circles to create a lovely and pleasing scale-like repeating pattern.

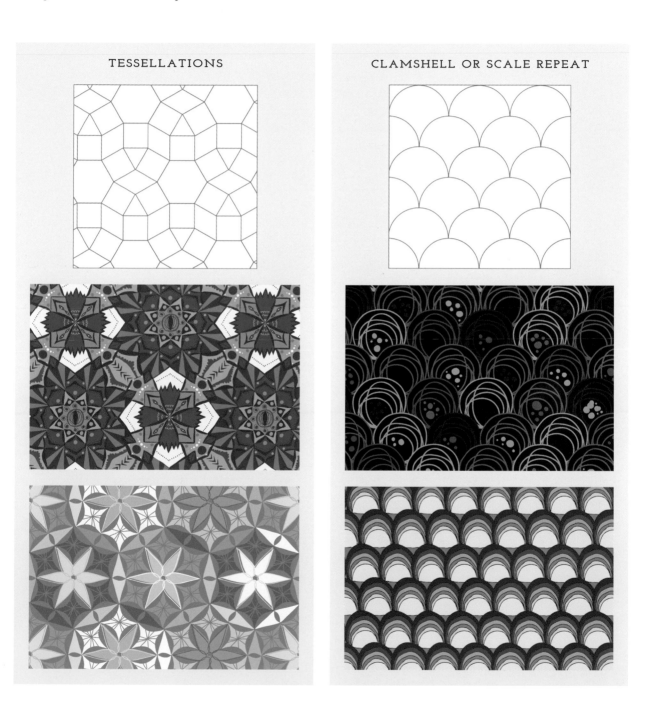

TESSELLATIONS

CLAMSHELL OR SCALE REPEAT

LAYOUT AND SYMMETRY

How you choose to lay out the motifs within your design will also affect how your pattern looks. Your designs can be structured or they can be laid out in a more organic way – both are lovely.

STRUCTURED LAYOUTS (OR SET LAYOUTS)

A structured layout will often give your pattern more of a repetitive and geometric feel. This does not mean you must use geometric motifs in a set layout – you could just as easily use quirky graphics, flowers, words or anything else. But the way those quirky graphics, flowers or words will repeat will appear more structured.

RANDOM LAYOUTS

Random layouts will give your patterns an organic feeling of being scattered all over the place. Motifs are generally evenly spaced, and the repeats are not supposed to be obvious, as they can sometimes be in a design with a set layout.

STRUCTURED OR SET LAYOUTS

RANDOM LAYOUTS

SYMMETRY

For a design to repeat properly, it must be symmetrical. This means is that anything overlapping the edges of your pattern tile must repeat at exactly the correct distance on the opposite side of the tile. Otherwise, your pattern will not repeat correctly and will therefore have a noticeable seam where the pattern does not match up with itself.

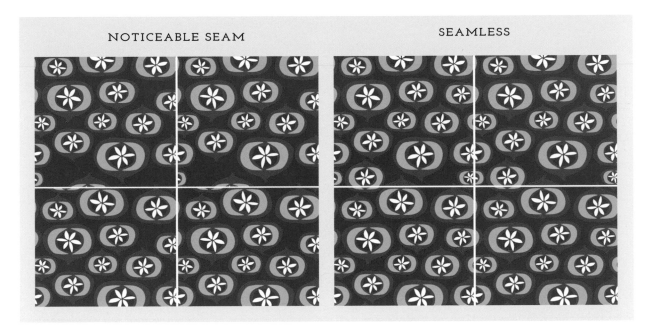

Follow the Arrow swing tags by Toodles Noodles. Photo by Eleanor at JEL.

DIRECTION AND ORIENTATION

A pattern can be either directional or non-directional in its orientation. The direction refers to the number of different ways you can rotate a pattern in 90° turns while the look of the design remains the same.

DIRECTIONAL PATTERNS

These can be viewed in either one direction or two; these are called one-way prints and two-way prints. It is common for novelty prints to be either one-way or two-way, because of the recognisable nature of the motifs.

NON-DIRECTIONAL PATTERNS

These can be viewed in four directions and are called four-way prints or tossed prints. The two names are frequently used interchangeably, but technically four-way prints involve motifs laid out in a geometric fashion in four directions so the pattern looks the same only when rotated at 90°-turns. The motifs in tossed prints are laid out in any direction so the pattern can be rotated in any angle and still appear the same.

DIRECTIONAL PATTERNS

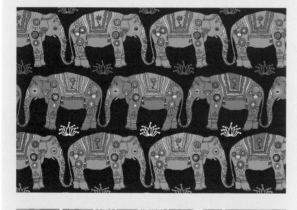

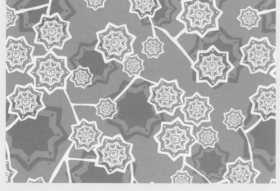

NON-DIRECTIONAL PATTERNS

SCALE AND SPACING

Scale and spacing are not only important stylistic choices,
but they are also important considerations when you
have specific uses in mind for your designs.

SCALE

Scale refers to the sise of the motifs within a
pattern design. They can range from quite tiny,
such as a tiny polka dot pattern, to quite large,
such as a bold, graphic floral wallpaper pattern.
You should consider the scale of your design if
you have a specific end use in mind. For example,
when designing a motif for a card, keep it small so
you can fit a lot of the pattern onto the card. If
you're designing wallpaper, the details in a small
motif will be lost when viewed from afar.

SPACING

Spacing refers to how closely the motifs within
a pattern are placed. Your patterns can leave
large swathes of background showing or none at
all, or you can place them somewhere in between.
Patterns in which the motifs are close together,
with not much background, are called allover
patterns. Allover patterns can be large or small
in scale. Ditsies are allover patterns made up of
tiny motifs, often floral or novelty in nature.

Chapter Four
MAKING PATTERNS

It's time for the fun to begin. These practical tutorials will teach you several different techniques for creating a motif, as well as how to turn those motifs into the three different types of repeating patterns (a straight repeat, a half-drop repeat and a brick repeat). You'll learn how to create a single motif using a variety of techniques, which you can then use to create a simple, single-motif repeating pattern. Then you'll learn how to take these techniques to the next level and apply them to creating a more complex pattern tile.

At the foundation of every pattern is a grid of rectangles or squares repeated in a specific way. This rectangle, when filled with motifs, is your pattern tile. The pattern tile can contain just one motif or many, but this grid lies at the basis of every type of pattern.

Additionally, you'll learn the basics of how to turn your pattern tiles in to seamless repeating patterns using computer design software. The central focus of this book is to create patterns by hand, but the tutorial should give you a good start and a solid base for experimenting with your own digital patterns and then, if you choose to, you can try out your digital pattern expertise on the cyanotype pattern-making tutorial.

Smartphone cases pattern designed by Jessica Swift for Case-Mate.
Photo by Jessica Nichols.

DESIGNING A MOTIF

A motif can be as simple as a dot, as complicated as twisting, intertwining vines and flowers, or anything in between. There are absolutely no rules about what constitutes a motif.

The motifs created for the hand-printing projects in this book are mainly simple and bold geometric graphics, to best demonstrate in a clear way some basic techniques and ways to create patterns. Take these skills and practice, embellish and build upon them. The projects are designed to be stepping stones in your own creative development as a pattern designer.

One of the simplest ways to explore motifs for possible use in your patterns is in your sketchbook. Doodling is rich ground for motif development. If you draw a motif you love in your sketchbook, an easy way to replicate it onto different surfaces is using carbon transfer paper.

A motif can be used alone, to create a single-motif pattern, or you can combine them within a pattern to create a more complex design. One way is not better than the other; they are just different ways of using motifs to create beautiful patterns.

It's important to note that both single-motif patterns and more complex patterns with multiple motifs are built on the same type of rectangular grid. As you begin to choose what will make up your pattern, begin to imagine how they will fit into a rectangle, to make up your pattern tile. Your pattern tile would consist of simply one motif when creating a single-motif pattern; if using multiple motifs in your pattern, your pattern tile will contain all of those motifs arranged in some configuration. The principles are the same no matter how simple or complex the motifs you use.

When picturing a pattern tile in my mind, I find it helps to think of beautifully patterned ceramic tiles, such as those from Italy or Morocco. The patterns on these tiles repeat endlessly, but they

Left: Liett pattern, straight repeat.
Right: Olga pattern, tossed straight repeat.

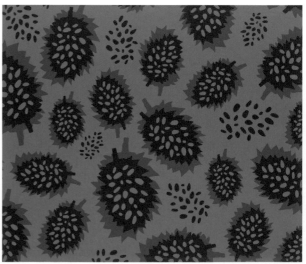

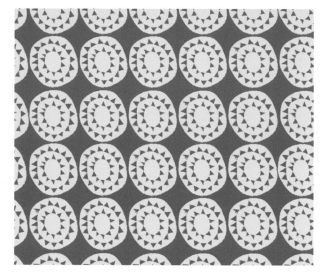

give you the advantage of being able to see the seams. When creating your own designs, it might be helpful in the beginning to visualise placing your motifs onto real tiles. Imagine three tiles in a straight line, and a motif slightly larger than the space on the tile. When you place your motif onto the first tile in the row, look to see what overlaps onto the next tile and where your pattern starts again. Does your motif need some tweaks or can you see how you create the repeat? Can you now see clearly what the pattern tile is made of?

Clockwise: Visual illustration of how pattern tiles work. Shalimar pattern, tossed straight repeat. Santoosh pattern, tossed straight repeat. Tamm pattern, straight repeat.

USING CARBON TRANSFER PAPER
- Place a sheet of transfer paper, carbon side down, on top of the surface onto which you'd like to transfer your motif.
- Place your drawing face up on top of the carbon paper, and trace over it with a pen or pencil.
- Repeat the process in rows to create a repeating pattern.

SALT

CHAMPIGNON

CREATING A REPEAT

Now it's time to take your motifs and turn them into a repeating pattern.
These tutorials will teach you how to create by hand the three main types
of repeat patterns: Straight repeats, half-drop repeats and brick repeats,
to create complex pattern tiles that will repeat seamlessly.

Repeating patterns are built upon a foundation of pattern tiles, arranged in specific configurations. No matter what motifs are in your pattern tile, you must arrange them properly in order for the pattern to work. This holds true whether you are creating your repeating pattern on paper or on a computer.

Pattern tiles can be made of one single motif or multiple motifs. Just as you can create a stencil in the shape of a flower, you can also create a stencil that is a complex square filled with flowers, based on the methods in these tutorials. Both will repeat using the same underlying grid pattern. The key to creating a pattern tile that repeats seamlessly is to make sure the elements that overlap the edges pick up in exact alignment on the opposite side.

STRAIGHT HALF-DROP BRICK

Opposite: Champignon fabric design by Zoe Ingram.

STRAIGHT REPEAT PATTERNS

Step 1

Cut a square or rectangular piece of paper to any sise. Begin drawing your motif in the middle of the page, staying away from the edges. You'll be cutting this page into four quadrants, so label each corner with a letter, A, B, C and D. Use a pencil so you can make changes as you go, if necessary.

Step 2

Measuring exactly halfway down the vertical length of your square or rectangle, cut horizontally, right through the centre. Don't worry if you cut right through shapes. They'll all match up in the end.

Step 3

Move section A-B to below C-D, butt the adjoining edges so the bottom piece is now at the top. Tape the back side of the pieces together in this new configuration.

Step 4

The horizontal centre of your newly arranged square or rectangle will be noticeably blank at this point. Fill in this centre horizontal space with more motifs; you can draw right over the seam in the middle. Stay away from the left and right sides of the square.

Step 5

Draw a vertical line down the centre of the square or rectangle. Cut along the line.

Step 6

Move the left side piece (D-B) to the right of piece C-A and tape the back side of the pieces together in this new arrangement.

Step 7

The vertical centre of your newly arranged square will now have some blank spots. Fill in this centre vertical space with more motifs, again drawing over the centre seam.

If any areas at the top and bottom centre of your design still look blank, simply untape the top and bottom half and switch their places again. This will create a small blank area in the centre of your design. Re-tape the two halves in the new configuration, and draw more motifs in the centre.

Drafting tape or dots will allow you to remove and re-stick the pieces without tearing the paper; another option is to cut through the taped edges with a craft knife.

Step 8

Your repeat is now complete. You can check it by tracing or photocopying your design four times and lining the quadrants up next to each other to see how your repeat works. You can also arrange the quadrants in a straight line, and the repeat will work that way, too.

SEE ALSO Motif styles, p. 30; Pattern types, p. 34

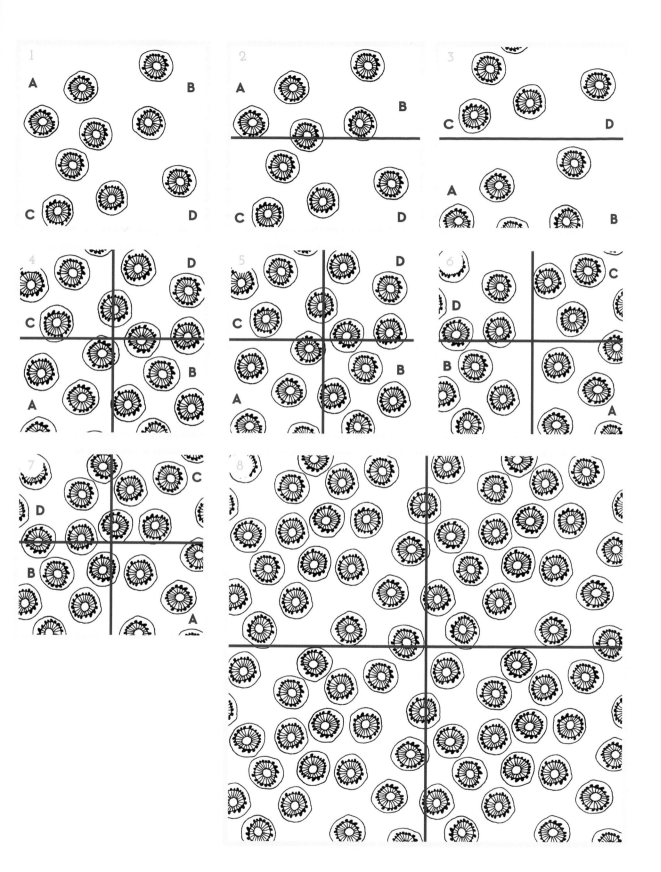

HALF-DROP REPEAT PATTERNS

BEFORE YOU BEGIN

The first four steps of this process are the same as for straight repeats. The only difference in creating a straight repeat and a half-drop repeat is the way you arrange your quadrants. Pay attention to step 6 in particular.

Step 1

Draw your motifs onto a square or rectangle using a pencil. Stay away from the edges and label each corner with a letter, A, B, C and D.

Step 2

Measure halfway across the horizontal length of the page, and cut vertically, through the centre of your square.

Step 3

Move section A–B to below C–D, butt the adjoining edges so the bottom piece is now at the top. Tape the back side of the pieces together in this new configuration.

Step 4

The horizontal centre of your newly arranged square will be blank. Fill in the centre space with more motifs; drawing right over this new seam in the middle. Stay away from the left and right sides of the page.

Step 5

Measure exactly halfway across the horizontal width of your page and cut through your square vertically this time. Then cut the four quadrants apart.

Step 6

Move the pieces D and B to the left of C and A. Here is the crucial step: switch the position of the two pieces on the right. Piece A goes to the top and piece C goes to the bottom. The top right piece is now on the bottom right and the bottom right piece is now on the top right.

Step 7

Tape the four quadrants together on the back side in this new configuration. Draw more motifs in the blank vertical seam area.

Step 8

Cut along the horizontal seam, and move piece D–A to below piece B–C. Fill in any white central space with more motifs.

Step 9

Cut along the horizontal and vertical seams and move the quadrants back to their original configuration. You can check your pattern by tracing or photocopying your design four times and lining the quadrants up in a half-drop formation to see how your repeat works.

SEE ALSO Layout and symmetry, p. 40; Direction and orientation, p. 42

Tutorial
BRICK REPEAT PATTERNS

The process for creating a brick repeat is the same as for a half-drop, but with your paper rotated 90°, so all your vertical cuts and movements are not horizontal, and vice versa.

Step 1

Draw your motifs onto a square or rectangle using a pencil. Stay away from the edges. Label each corner with A, B, C and D.

Step 2

Measure halfway across the horizontal length of the page, and cut vertically, through the centre of your square.

Step 3

Move section A–C to the right of B–D, butt the adjoining edges so the left piece is now on the right. Tape the back side of the pieces together in this new configuration.

Step 4

The vertical centre of your newly arranged square will now be blank. Fill in this centre vertical space with more motifs, drawing over the seam in the middle.

Step 5

Measure exactly halfway down the vertical width of your page and cut through your square horizontally this time. Then cut all four quadrants apart.

Step 6

Move the top two pieces (B and A) to the bottom position and the bottom pieces (D and C) to the top. Here is the crucial step: switch the position of the two pieces (B and A) on the bottom. The bottom left piece is now on the bottom right and the bottom right piece is now on the bottom left.

Step 7

Tape the four quadrants together on the back side in this new configuration. Fill in the blank horizontal seam area if needed with more motifs.

Step 8

Cut the pieces apart vertically and move the left pieces (C and B) to the right of pieces D and A. Fill in any blank central space with more motifs.

Step 9

Cut apart all the quadrants, and move them back to their original configuration. You can check it by tracing or photocopying your design four times and lining the quadrants up in a half-drop formation to see how your repeat works.

SEE ALSO Sourcing ideas for patterns, p. 18

Tutorial
RUBBER BLOCK STAMPS

Rubber block printing is a great way to create a hand-printed repeat pattern. Making your own stamps is quite addictive, and you might be surprised to discover how easy it is. Linoleum and wood are a couple of other materials that are often used to make stamps, but rubber is by far the easiest to carve.

BEFORE YOU BEGIN

- Choose motifs without too many fine details; small lines can be challenging.
- When creating your motif, think in two dimensions: the surface (what will print) and the negative space (what won't print). Try creating motifs for stamps in black ink on white paper. There should be no shading in your motif.
- Use a light hand when carving - you can always go over your carved lines multiple times to deepen them. Trying to carve too deeply from the start can gouge the block and ruin your stamp. Your lines only need to be 1-3 millimetres ($\frac{1}{16}$-$\frac{1}{8}$ in) deep to work well.

Step 1
Draw your motif onto a blank rubber block with a pencil or pen (or transfer it from paper using the carbon transfer paper).

Step 2
Before carving, think through which areas of your motif will be carved away. Mark the rubber block if that's helpful.

Step 3
Start from the outer lines of the stamp and work inwards. Using very light pressure and holding your carving tool at a 45°-angle, carve around the outer lines of your motif.

Step 4
Carve around all the areas of negative space that you will eventually cut away.

Step 5
Carve out the negative space until all that remains is the raised shape of your motif.

Step 6
Using a craft knife, cut away excess rubber around your motif.

Step 7
Rinse with water or brush away any stray bits of rubber clinging to the stamp.

SEE ALSO Stamping cards and envelopes, p. 100; Printing on tiles, p. 126

WHAT YOU'LL NEED

- Pencil or pen
- Rubber printing block for carving
- Carbon transfer paper
- Carving tool
- Craft knife

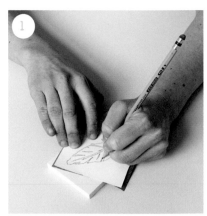

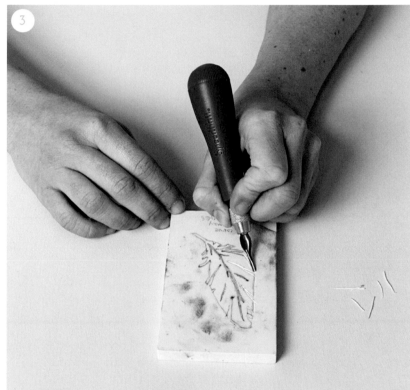

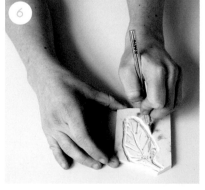

FOAM STAMPS

Foam stamps are great fun to make. The process is quick and easy, and the stamps are great for printing because you can see exactly where and how you're placing your motif through the clear acrylic block.

BEFORE YOU BEGIN

- Choose motifs without too many fine line details for foam stamps. Small lines can be quite challenging to carve with a craft knife.
- Think about foam stamps in two dimensions. You will cut the negative space away from your foam with a craft knife or scissors, so what remains will be the stamp's surface.
- Your motif can be one connected piece, or you can cut it out in separate pieces and reassemble them on your acrylic block. Either way will work.

Step 1

Draw your motif onto the foam sheet with a pencil or pen (or transfer it from paper using the carbon transfer paper).

Step 2

Before cutting, think through which areas of your motif will be negative space and which will be cut away. Mark the foam sheet if that's helpful.

Step 3

Start from the inside and work outwards. Starting with the innermost sections of your motif, use a craft knife to begin carefully cutting away the areas of negative space.

Step 4

Work your way outwards, cutting away all the negative space and cutting the final outer stamp shape out of the foam. You should have one stamp piece (or several, depending on your motif design) that is separate from the sheet of foam. Refine any rough edges using your craft knife or scissors.

Step 5

Carefully spray the face up side of your foam motif pieces with spray adhesive.

Step 6

Carefully place your acrylic block directly on top of the sprayed pieces. Press firmly to adhere. Your stamp is now ready for inking and printing.

SEE ALSO Foam stamping a tote bag, p. 78; Foam stamping gift wrap, p. 90

WHAT YOU'LL NEED

- Pencil or pen
- Sheet of craft foam, any colour
- Carbon transfer paper
- Craft knife
- Scissors
- Spray adhesive
- Clear acrylic block

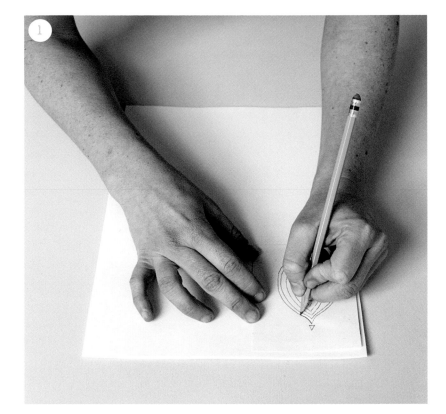

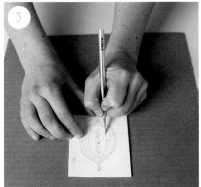

Tutorial
STENCILS

Before I learned how to make repeat patterns using a computer, stencils were one of my go-to methods for creating shapes I could easily duplicate. Stencils can be made out of many different materials, such as acetate, cardboard, mount board, cardstock, adhesive paper, and grease proof paper. We're going to learn to create an acetate stencil, but you can adapt these instructions for use with any other material.

Text acetate, or transparency film, is just a fancy name for a piece of thin plastic. It comes in rolls or sheets in varying thicknesses. Acetate is easy to cut with a craft knife or scissors, it is flexible, and will last a long time if you take care of it. It's the perfect material for stencil-making.

BEFORE YOU BEGIN

- Cutting a stencil must be approached differently to carving a stamp. The areas you cut away are the areas that will print. Because you're cutting and not carving, your motif will not be attached to any sort of backing. This means you must be mindful of how the pieces of your motif will connect to one another in order not to be cut away completely.
- Bold graphics without too many details tend to work well for stencils.

Step 1
Draw a motif on paper and place it underneath a sheet of acetate. Tape down the edges of the acetate so it's firmly attached to the paper.

Step 2
Trace the motif onto the acetate using a permanent marker, following the outlines of your motif. Use the paper underneath as a guide.

Step 3
Remove the paper motif and cut out the acrylic tracing using a craft knife, being mindful of pieces without attachment points that may mistakenly be cut away. (Add small attachment points as you go if necessary.)

Step 4
Untape your stencil when you've finished cutting and cut it out of the larger sheet of acetate. Your stencil is finished.

SEE ALSO Stencilling on a paper bag, p. 114; Stencilling a border on a wall, p. 124

WHAT YOU'LL NEED

- Pencil or pen
- Sketchbook or loose-leaf paper
- Cutting surface (sheet of card, mount board, or a self-adhesive cutting mat)
- Sheet of acetate
- Masking tape
- Permanent marker
- Craft knife

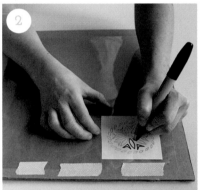

Tutorial
SIMPLE SILK SCREENS

Silk-screening can seem intimidating with talk about exposures and emulsifiers and dark rooms; it's not the most inviting process for a newcomer to pattern making. This method, though, couldn't be easier. Totally gratifying and satisfying, it's foolproof screen printing for all.

BEFORE YOU BEGIN

- Leave about 5 centimetres (2 inches) of room around your motif at each edge of the screen. This is to leave room for squeegee and ink.
- If any ink dries in your screen, the screen will be ruined. Be sure to rinse out your screen gently with cool water immediately after you have finished printing to keep it clean and unclogged.
- Scrubbing your screen could cause the screen filler to fade and become damaged. Always rinse your screen gently, and it should last a long time.
- Be sure to paint your screen filler onto the recessed side of your screen – this will ensure nice, flat contact between the screen and the surface when you start printing.
- The areas that are painted with screen filler fluid will not print. The areas that are not painted with screen filler fluid will print.

Step 1

Draw your motif onto the screen with a pencil or apply using transfer paper.

Step 2

Before painting the screen filler fluid onto the screen, think through which areas of your motif will be printed with ink and which areas will be negative space.

Step 3

Shake or stir your screen filler fluid. Holding your screen and using a paintbrush, fill in all the areas of negative space around your motif with a very thin coat of screen filler fluid. Remember: Everything you coat with screen filler will not print.

Step 4

Lay the screen flat, evenly propped around the frame so it doesn't stick to your surface, and let this layer dry; you can speed this process by using a hairdryer or heat gun. Paint two to three thin layers of screen filler, letting each dry before applying the next.

Step 5

Hold your screen up to the light. Any areas or pinholes that were missed within the screen filler areas will print through. Fill in any missed areas with a thin layer of screen filler. Let the screen dry overnight before using.

SEE ALSO Screen printing a Furoshiki, p. 76

PLANNING PATTERNS

WHAT YOU'LL NEED

- Pencil
- Paper
- Carbon transfer paper
- Pre-stretched silk screen
- Screen filler fluid
- Paintbrushes in various sizes
- Hairdryer or heat gun (o)

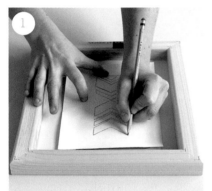

MAKING YOUR PATTERN DIGITAL

Digitising the pattern tiles you created by hand is possible in both Adobe Photoshop and Adobe Illustrator. These are two digital image editing software programs which allow you to create your repeating pattern designs with a computer. You can work with your hand-drawn tiles directly once scanned, or you can use them as guides to trace over digitally within the program you choose to use. If you worked in pencil, trace over your design with black pen or marker and then scan your artwork into your computer at the highest resolution possible. Save as a high quality JPEG or a TIFF file at 300 dots per inch (dpi) or higher.

MAKING YOUR PATTERN DIGITAL IN PHOTOSHOP

Step 1

Open your scanned file in Photoshop. Crop the image.

Step 2

Clean up any unwanted lines or spots with the Eraser tool. Convert to Greyscale.

Step 3

Take note of your image size in pixels (px). To test (and repair) the repeat, go to the Filter menu and choose Offset. Set the vertical measurement to 0 (zero) and the horizontal measurement to half the width of your file. (The file in the diagram is 2400 px wide, set to 1200 px.) This brings the top and bottom edges of your file together in the centre. Use the tools in Photoshop to repair your design if needed. (For example, you can see that the file had a grey line running through the centre that was covered over using the Paintbrush tool.)

Step 4

Repeat the Offset procedure (see step 3), but this time set your vertical measurement to half the height of your file (1200 px again) and the horizontal measurement to 0 (zero). This brings the left and right edges together in the centre. Make any repairs needed.

Step 5

Set both of your Offset filters to 0 (zero) to bring the design back to its original configuration. (If you forget this step, it's fine - your repeat will still work properly.) Your file is now in perfect repeat and ready to be coloured. To turn it into a pattern swatch, go to Edit > Define Pattern. Name your pattern. With the Paint Bucket tool selected, click on the Fill Area Source dropdown menu at the top left of the Tool Bar. Select Pattern, which is where you will find your pattern swatch.

Step 6

Create a large new Photoshop file. Using the Paint Bucket tool, click anywhere inside your new file to fill it with your pattern.

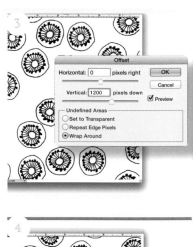

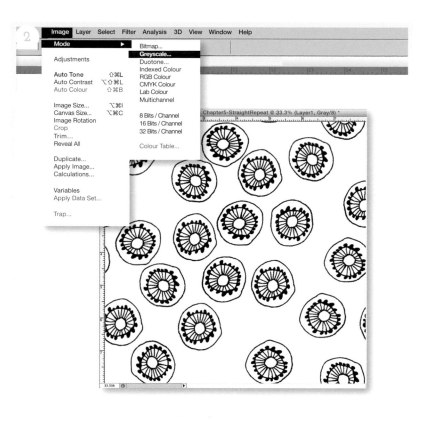

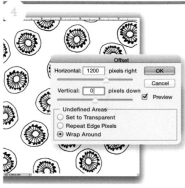

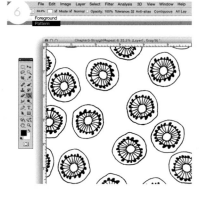

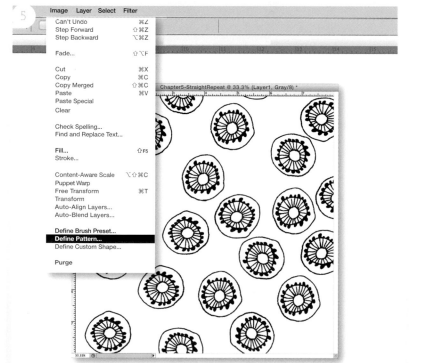

MAKING YOUR PATTERN DIGITAL IN ILLUSTRATOR

Step 1

Create a new file and place (File > Place) your scanned artwork into the artboard in perfect alignment. For example, if your scanned artwork is 20 x 20 centimetres (8 x 8 in), your file should also be this size.

Step 2

With your artwork selected, click the small arrow next to the Live Trace button in the Tool Bar at the top of the Illustrator window (or for the same options go to: Object > Live Trace > Tracing Options). Select the line quality you prefer from the Live Trace options. (Start with the Lettering setting.)

Step 3

Click on the Expand button in the Tool Bar at the top of the Illustrator window (or go to: Object > Live Trace > Expand).

Step 4

Ungroup your design (Object > Ungroup). This means you can click on different pieces of your motif separately.

Step 5

To make sure your repeat works, move any pieces that overlap the top edge down to the bottom edge (Object > Transform > Move). Adjust if the motifs don't match up.

Step 6

Select one motif from the bottom and group the two pieces together (Object > Group). Repeat this with each motif.

Step 7

Select all the bottom motifs and copy them back up to the top, using the Move tool again (Object > Transform > Move). To move pieces up, use a negative number. Click the Copy button instead of the OK button this time. Your top and bottom motifs should now match up perfectly.

Step 8

Follow steps 5 to 7 for the left and right sides of your design. Instead of moving the Vertical distance, this time change the Horizontal number.

Step 9

To make it a repeating tile, create a blank square the exact size of your artboard using the Rectangle tool. Move it to the very back layer of your design (Object > Arrange > Send to Back).

Step 10

Select everything on your artboard, including the blank rectangle in the back. Go to Edit > Define Pattern. Name your pattern and click OK. It will now show up in your Swatches Palette.

Step 11

To test it, create a rectangle larger than your artboard, off to one side. Click on the pattern swatch you just created to fill the square, and watch it magically fill the square with your repeating pattern.

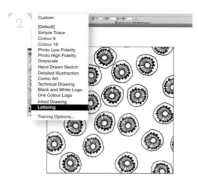

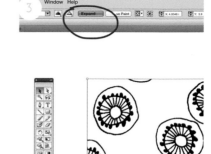

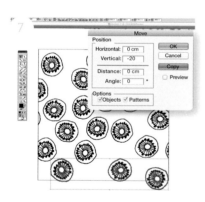

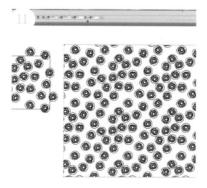

PREPARING TO CYANOTYPE

A cyanotype is a type of photographic print that produces a beautiful blue image.
If you are familiar with what an architectural blueprint looks like, you've seen a cyanotype.

The beauty of the cyanotype process is that it can be used for more than reproducing diagrams and plans - it's also an amazing and simple way to use the digital images you just learned to how to make to create gorgeous pattern designs of your very own! As well as creating patterns using your new digital skills, you can use this process to print natural and simple patterns too - almost anything can be used to create an image and you could even use a photograph you have taken as your pattern tile, for example. This page gives you all the information to prepare to cyanotype print. For the printing method, turn to page 88.

Step 1

You will need to create a digital negative of your artwork. Using the techniques in the Making your pattern digital tutorial (see pp. 64-67), design a pattern tile (it must be in black only!) and make it digital.

Step 2

Print your digital pattern onto clear transparency film on a laser printer, and you are ready to begin!

Step 3

Alternatively, use an opaque black marker to draw an image onto transparency film if you would prefer to make your patterns by hand. Or you can use objects, like lace or leaves, to create more organic patterns.

Now you're ready to cyanotype print! For instructions on how to make your own cyanotype paper, see page 88.

BEFORE YOU BEGIN

- Remember that whatever fabric or paper is covered and is not exposed to direct sunlight will not change colour.
- As well as printing a digital pattern tile onto a sheet of clear transparency film, you can create a pattern by hand by printing or drawing images onto clear transparency film.
- Print onto your transparency film with a laser printer. Inkjet printers tend not to return good results as the ink coverage is not as dense.

SEE ALSO Making your pattern digital, p. 64; Sourcing ideas for patterns, p. 18

WHAT YOU'LL NEED

- Clear transparency film
- Digital pattern tile
- Opaque black marker (o)
- Objects such as lace or leaves (o)

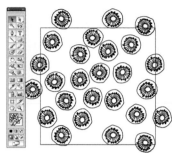

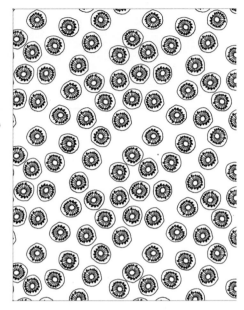

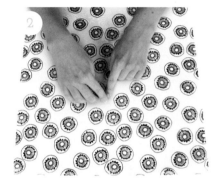

Section Two

USING PATTERNS

Chapter Five

FABRIC

I've loved fabric ever since I was a little girl. My mum made dolls and always had piles and piles of beautiful, colourful fabric on hand. My grandmother was a quilter and had even more piles of fabric than my mum did. Fabric is in my bones! It gives me great joy to design fabric now as an adult and to get to see my own fabric mixed into those gorgeous piles in my mum's sewing room.

Before I started designing fabric for digital printing, I hand-printed everything from napkins and place mats to eco-friendly gift wrap (called Furoshiki) and clothing. It's a fun, meditative and deeply satisfying process. Mistakes and printing imperfections are practically unavoidable, which gives the finished products a special charm and personality that is not present in digitally-printed fabric. The items you create will be truly one of a kind!

Before you get started, a trip to a local fabric shop could be an inspirational and educational outing - browsing the shop's aisles will give you endless ideas for the colour and motif choices in your own patterns. Fabric shops are also a fantastic place to study different kinds of patterns, work out how they're created and to really get a feel for the massive variety of different types of designs that the term 'repeat pattern' encompasses. It is truly a magnificently broad term!

Once you begin, I think your mind will start spinning with the possibilities that hand-printing on fabric hold: skirt hems, tote bags, table runners, baby items, handmade dolls! The only limit with this versatile technique is your own imagination.

Screen-printed fabric by Jessica Swift. Photo by Jessica Nichols.

APPLYING PATTERNS TO FABRIC

The tutorials in this chapter are some of my favourites.
Fabric is so versatile and lends itself to many different types
of printing and so many different uses.

On the following pages you'll learn how to screen print a two-way design onto fabric to create a Furoshiki: a beautiful, reusable and eco-friendly alternative to paper gift wrap that originated in Japan. You'll also learn how you can use a foam stamp to print a seamless half-drop pattern onto a tote bag. This technique can just as easily apply to printing onto a table runner, a skirt hem, a T-shirt or anything else you'd like to adorn.

Motifs within a pattern tile can be laid out in simple or complex arrangements and can be configured to repeat in straight, half-drop or brick formations. Any and all of these styles and techniques are applicable for printing on fabric. Multiple options always exist for making a project simpler or more challenging.

It's important to do test prints before beginning to print your projects, so having extra fabric, tote bags or other materials on hand is a good idea. With screen printing especially, you'll want to make sure you've got the hang of it before setting out to print on your final surface; it can take a few attempts to get the correct pressure for the squeegee and to figure out your rhythm.

Explore printing on fabric using the other methods: potato stamping, stencilling and rubber block printing. You could even get yourself some fabric paint and simply hand paint a pattern onto fabric with gorgeous results! Imagine using this technique on a silk scarf . . . beautiful. There are so many options.

Screen-printed fabric by Jessica Swift. Photo by Jessica Nichols.

Screen-printed Rough Cuts pile **(from top to bottom):** Pebble in Pollen, Smudge and Lollipop, Woodpile in Spruce and Pollen, and Rough Diamond in Sunny Day, Lollipop and Inkspot colourways by Skinny laMinx. Photo by Heather Moore.

SCREEN PRINTING A FUROSHIKI

Step 1

Tape down some scrap paper or a piece of cardboard onto your work surface to protect it from ink that may bleed through as you print. Lay the fabric flat on the scrap paper and secure the edges and four corners with masking tape. Place the screen face down on top of the fabric. Any starting place is fine.

Step 2

Spoon a line of ink onto your screen, directly above the design.

Step 3

Hold the screen down firmly with one hand. Hold the squeegee in your other hand. Place the squeegee at a 45°-angle on the screen above the line of ink. Pull the ink down firmly and steadily over the image until it is evenly covered with ink.

Step 4

Lift the screen to see your first print.

Step 5

While the screen is lifted, use your squeegee to pull the ink upwards so the line of ink is again at the top of your screen. This step is important. Ink that dries in your screen will be permanent, so you'll want to keep it 'flooded' with a thin layer of ink between each printing.

Step 6

Place the screen face down on the fabric again, taking care not to lay the screen on any freshly printed areas. Pull the ink down again, as in step 3.

Step 7

Repeat steps 4 to 7, printing the motifs in any configuration you like(in this tutorial we have created a 2-way repeat). When needed, spoon more ink in a line above the motif on the screen. Print the motif in two directions by flipping your screen 180° and printing some of your motifs upside down.

Step 8

Clean your screen with cold water immediately after printing and air dry.

Step 9

Let the fabric dry fully (using a hairdryer or a heat gun can speed this up), then continue printing your motifs to fill any blank areas created while avoiding the areas of wet ink. Clean the screen with cold water again when finished printing. Repeat steps 8 and 9 as needed.

Step 10

Once the fabric is completely dry, it is ready to use in your beautiful, eco-friendly gift-wrapping projects!

SEE ALSO Backgrounds and borders, p. 32; Simple silk screens, p. 62

WHAT YOU'LL NEED

- Scrap paper or cardboard
- Masking tape
- Any squares of fabric larger than motif
- Screen with motif (see p. 62)
- Screenprinting ink
- Old spoon
- Squeegee
- Hairdryer/heat gun (o)

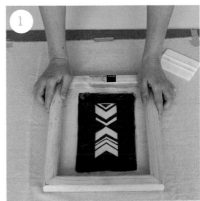

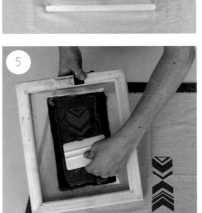

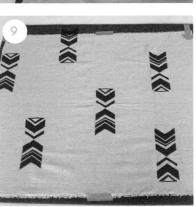

Tutorial
FOAM STAMPING A TOTE BAG

TOP TIP

• Heat set the ink to prevent the tote bag from fading when washed by placing a piece of fabric or a towel on top of the tote bag and ironing it thoroughly on both sides.

Step 1

Place the cardboard inside the tote bag to protect against printing through thin or porous fabric to the other side of the tote bag. Lay the tote bag on a flat surface. Squeeze ink onto your palette and roll your brayer through it until it's coated evenly with a thin layer of ink. Roll the brayer over the surface of your stamp.

Step 2

If there are any portions of the bag that you don't want to print or that you want to protect from ink, cover them with masking tape. Place a sheet of scrap paper underneath the tote bag when printing over the edges, to protect your work surface from ink.

Step 3

In this project, we are creating a complex half-drop repeat pattern, so to do this start at the top left corner of the bag. Place the foam stamp face down and press firmly for several seconds. Lift the stamp.

Step 4

Place the left edge of your motif directly underneath the bottom edge of your last printed stamp; press firmly and lift stamp. Repeat down to finish the column. Reapply ink to your stamp when the layer of ink on your stamp's surface is no longer consistent.

Step 5

To print the second row, begin to the right of the first column at the top of the tote bag. Position the stamp halfway down the length of the print in the top left corner, so the motifs in the half-drop repeat match up. Continue printing vertically down the column to the bottom of the bag; the entire row should be staggered halfway with the first column.

Step 6

Begin the third column in the same upper position as the first column. Stagger alternating rows, so every other row is printed halfway with the previous column, making sure the motifs match up. Repeat steps 2 to 6, printing in columns to cover the entire surface of the bag. The half-drop pattern tile stamp will have created a lovely and complex repeating design.

Step 7

Let the tote bag dry completely. Repeat steps 1 to 6 on the back of the bag. Once dry, your tote bag is ready to use!

SEE ALSO Half-drop repeat patterns, p. 52; Foam stamps, p. 58

WHAT YOU'LL NEED

- Blank tote bag
- Cardboard cut to fit tote (o)
- Block-printing ink, 1 colour
- Wax paper for ink
- Brayer
- Half-drop repeat foam stamp (see p. 52, p. 58)
- Masking tape (o)
- Scrap paper

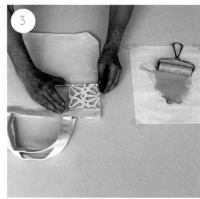

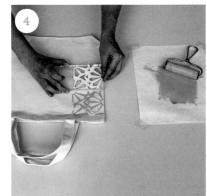

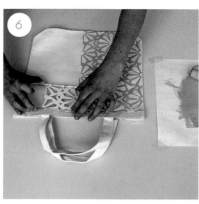

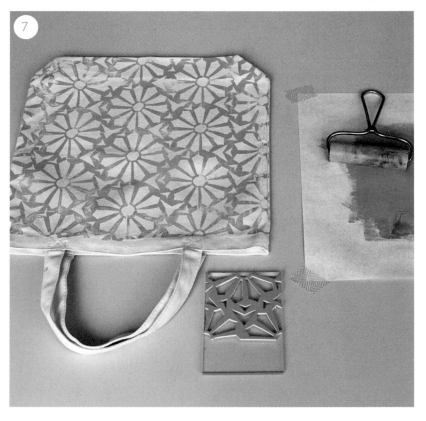

Interview
HITOMI KIMURA

PROFESSION: Fabric designer
COUNTRY: Japan

What is the inspiration behind your sophisticated, simplistic and beautiful pattern style?

I think my designs get inspiration from the simple lines of natural things. I also design geometric patterns, but most of the time I like to create designs where you can feel some kind of warmth by adding hand drawn touches.

What is your process for turning designs from your sketchbook into fabric patterns?

I usually pick up several motifs from my sketches and drawings to start with and experiment with various compositions and play around with them on my computer. If I like the design, I make a repeatable version of it by carefully positioning each motif. I also try to make a 'space' look nice. And I sometimes make the pattern as simple as possible by removing some of the motifs.

How do you choose your colour combinations?

I try as many variations as possible, both on my computer and with real materials. The

same colour scheme doesn't always look good on another design so I just keep searching for colourways I like by trial and error.

How does designing a pattern for a machine knit differ from designing patterns for digital printing on fabric?

Designing patterns for digital printing is so much fun and you could almost turn anything into patterns. You have such freedom. On the other hand, designing knitted fabric has more restrictions. And especially because my knitting machine uses an old punchcard system to generate a pattern, the number of stitches to be repeated is limited and I can design a straight repeating pattern only. But I like designing knit patterns for this reason too. I enjoy both freedom and restrictions.

What advice can you share with aspiring fabric designers?

I think experimenting a lot with various techniques and materials can be key to good designs. And don't be afraid to try a new style.

What is your favourite colour combination?

It's changing constantly, but at the moment I like coral pink and dark olive or pink and plum.

1: Hand screen-printed fabric;
2: Machine-knit cushion covers;
3: Hand screen-printed fabric;
4: Hand screen-printed cushions;
all by Hitomi Kimura.

GALLERY

Above: Emerald Triangle tote bag by Anna Joyce. Photo by Lisa Warninger. **Below:** Handmade dress from Dutch Love Fabric Collection by Susanne Firmenich, Hamburger Liebe. Photo by Susanne Firmenich. **Right:** Meadow stockings by Monaluna. Photo by Jennifer Moore.

Left: Handmade shirt dress from Fly Fabric Collection by Susanne Firmenich, Hamburger Liebe. Photo by Susanne Firmenich. **Below:** Handmade shirt from Tulipa Fabric Collection by Susanne Firmenich, Hamburger Liebe. Photo by Susanne Firmenich. **Bottom:** Urban Patch Fabric Collection by Monaluna. Photo by David Miguelucci.

[All images on this page are copyright to the producers and photographers. They are for inspiration only, and not for use in commercial projects.]

Chapter Six
GIFT WRAP

Is there anything better than a beautifully wrapped gift?

Making your own gift wrap is a fun and satisfying way to turn your motifs into repeats on a larger scale – the only thing to confine you is the size of your paper. There is no need to limit yourself to printing only on white paper; you can find rolls or sheets of coloured paper at art shops, stationers, hardware stores, or online. Rolls of brown packing paper, rosin paper, rice paper, graph paper and coloured watercolour paper are all fun options on which to try printing. Beware, hand-printing your own gift wrap is addictive – you may never want to buy gift wrap again.

What I find to be the most charming part of hand-printing is that no two prints ever turn out quite the same. The images will depend on how firmly you pressed the stamp, how much ink was on your roller, how long you exposed your image to the sun what type and texture of paper you're using. The inherent unpredictability and element of surprise that goes along with hand-printing will naturally infuse your projects with a lovely, appealing handmade quality and will ensure that each time you set stamp, brush or stencil to paper your results will be just a little bit different than before. That's all part of the fun!

Hand-printed gift wrap by Jessica Swift. Photo by Jessica Nichols.

APPLYING PATTERNS TO PAPER

There is something so pleasing and satisfying about
working with paper. Hand-printing on paper is quick, fun,
and obsession-inducing once you get the hang of it!

These tutorials will give you the confidence
and the know-how to create your own gorgeous,
hand-printed gift wrap. As you practice the
printing techniques, you can make the projects
more complicated by printing with multiple
colours, creating repeats that require more precise
measurement, combining multiple motifs in
one repeat and layering colours and motifs.

You can use many everyday objects as stamps
or stencils for printing onto paper. Potatoes, celery,
wine bottle corks, pencil erasers, leaves, chunks
of wood, the edge of a cup, linoleum blocks, doilies,
fingertips, stencils, letterpress blocks and anything
else you can think of that is carvable and/or
inkable are possible mediums for printing patterns.

Different types of printing will require different
types of ink. When using a stamp to create your
repeat, block-printing ink is the best choice. It is
thicker than acrylic paint or screen printing ink
and will give you a nice, consistent stamped
image with clean edges.

OTHER TECHNIQUES TO TRY

- **Spray paint.** Try spray painting through
  stencils, doilies, screen from an old screen
  door, cookie cutters or over things like leaves
  to create interesting repeats.
- **Finger-printed polka dots.** This is as simple
  as dipping your finger into a pot of paint.
  Dip, print and repeat! Other tools to make
  dots with include pencil erasers, pencil tips,
  chopsticks, shish kebab sticks and corks.
- **Leaf printing.** Paint the back of a leaf with
  a thin layer of acrylic paint using a foam
  roller. Place the leaf, paint side down, on
  your paper, cover with a sheet of scrap
  paper and roll over it with a brayer.
- **Eraser stamps.** Use your carving tool to
  carve a tiny stamp into an artist's eraser.
- **Freehand drawing.** Transfer a sketch
  repeatedly onto a larger sheet of paper
  using transfer paper. Colour the images
  using paint, markers, coloured pencils or ink.

All images here and opposite: Hand-printed gift wrap by Jessica Swift. Photos by Jessica Nichols.

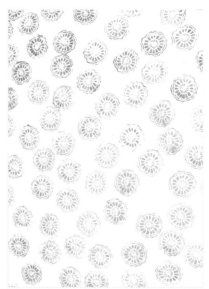

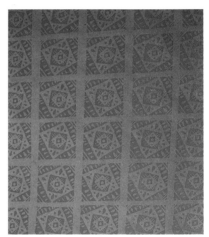

CYANOTYPE PRINTING ON PAPER

BEFORE YOU BEGIN
- For all the information you need to prepare your cyanotype print, see page 68.
- Please make sure you wear protective gloves throughout the process! The chemicals can be dangerous if not handled properly, and it's always good to be on the safe side.
- In this tutorial we have used a tossed straight repeat, but feel free to use any black repeating pattern

Step 1
Tape the sheet of drawing paper flat to the large piece of cardboard, securing the edges all the way around.

Step 2
In subdued light, mix a small amount of the cyanotype printing solution in the plastic mixing container according to the kit instructions.

Step 3
Still in subdued light, use a foam brush to coat the paper with a thin layer of the cyanotype printing solution. The paper will be a yellowish-green colour. Let dry in a dark room. (You can use a hairdryer if you'd like to speed up the drying time.)

Step 4
Using clear tape, attach the four transparency sheets with together so they form a seamless pattern.

Step 5
In subdued light, position the transparency sheets on top of the dry, coated paper. Place the sheet of glass or clear acrylic directly on top, ensuring the transparencies are pressed flat against the paper.

Step 6
Place in direct sunlight for 6 to 10 minutes. The colour will start to change from yellowish-green to slightly blue.

Step 7
Fill the large tub with 12-15 cm of water. Move the cyanotype in to subdued light, uncover and untape, and submerge the paper in the water for several minutes. The print will begin to turn blue!

Step 8
Add a capful of hydrogen peroxide to the water to speed up the oxidisation process. The print will become a darker, more saturated blue.

Step 9
Rinse the paper in fresh water, and hang to dry in subdued light. When fully dry, your paper is ready to use!

SEE ALSO Pattern types, p. 34; Preparing to cyanotype, p. 68

WHAT YOU'LL NEED

- Masking tape
- Large sheet of 45 x 60-cm (18 x 24-in) drawing paper
- Large piece of cardboard
- Protective gloves
- Cyanotype printing kit (see p. 137)
- Small plastic mixing container
- Small measuring cups
- Foam brush
- Hairdryer (o)
- Clear tape
- 4 sheets of 22 x 28-cm (8 x 11-in) transparency film printed with an 20 x 20-cm (8 x 8-in) black repeating pattern tile, trimmed to 20 x 20-cm (8 x 8-in)
- Sheet of glass or clear acrylic, 40 x 40 cm (16 x 16 in) or larger
- Large tub
- Water
- Hydrogen peroxide

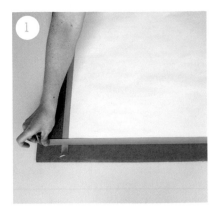

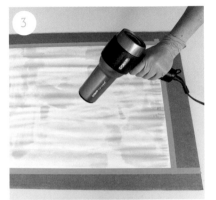

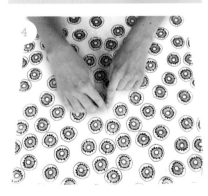

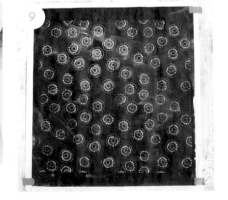

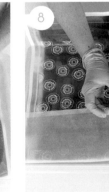

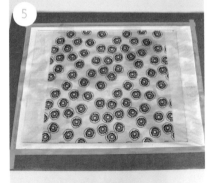

Tutorial
FOAM STAMPING GIFT WRAP

Step 1

Lay your paper out on a large flat surface and secure in position with masking tape. Squeeze ink onto your palette and roll your brayer through it until it's coated evenly with a thin layer of ink. Roll the brayer over the surface of your foam stamp, coating it evenly with a thin layer of ink.

Step 2

Place a sheet of scrap paper underneath your large sheet of paper when printing over the edges, to protect your flat surface from ink. Starting in the top left corner of your paper, place stamp face down and press firmly for several seconds. Lift the stamp.

Step 3

To create a straight repeat as we have here, then place the left edge of your stamp block immediately to the right of your last printed stamp; press firmly and lift stamp. Repeat across to finish the row.

Step 4

To print the second row, begin again on the left side of your paper. With your stamp in the same orientation as before, align the top edge with the bottom edge of the print in the top left corner. Repeat across the row.

Step 5

Repeat steps 1 to 4, moving down the page, until the paper is fully stamped.

SEE ALSO Choosing colours, p. 24; Foam stamps, p. 58

USING PATTERNS

WHAT YOU'LL NEED

- Large roll of paper
- Masking tape
- Block-printing ink
- Palette for ink
- Brayer
- Foam stamp (see p. 58)
- Sheets of scrap paper

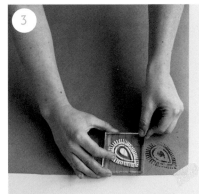

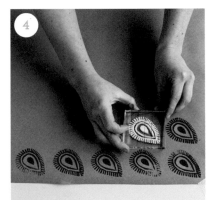

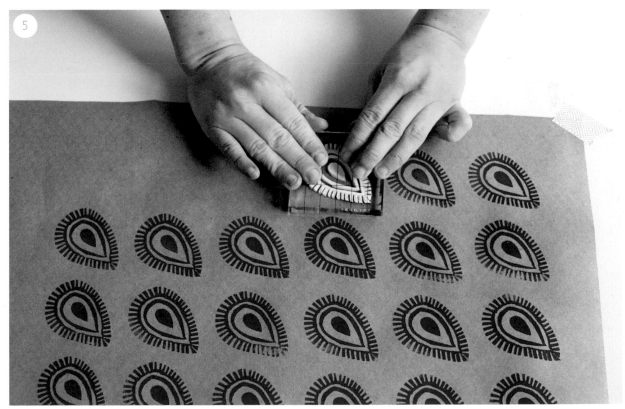

ZOE INGRAM

PROFESSION: Pattern designer
COUNTRY: Australia

How did you get your start as a pattern designer?

I graduated from the Scottish College of Textiles in 1997 with an honours degree in printed textiles. I fell in love with the process: The research; the initial drawing and investigating; then constructing a design; and finally preparing the screens, mixing dyes; and then printing. We did it all the old-fashioned way, by hand, in those days with no computers and I'm so glad I got to experience it. I had a 16-year break after I graduated – I feel as though I have come full circle now. My big break came in 2013 from Lilla Rogers and her amazing 'Make Art That Sells' class and the Global Talent Search competition, which I won. I am now represented by the Lilla Rogers Studio and, as part of the competition prize, I had the privilege of working with Robert Kaufman Fabrics (a dream job!) among other licencing deals. This is what I trained to do all those years ago and now I am lucky enough to be doing it.

What inspires you and how do you translate that into your work?

I am a 40-year-old woman but I still have my childlike imagination, which I never want to lose. That's really what I try to get across in my work. I love how my children are so free with their expressions, and the stories they tell me, as well as their lack of inhibition when they paint or draw remind me all the time to use my imagination. I love to try and get that sense of excitement, fun and happiness into my work. I'm also inspired a lot by my

3

1: Cuckoo clocks pattern;
2: Seedling plates;
3: Gift bag all by Zoe Ingram.
Photos by Zoe Ingram.

What advice can you share with someone who wants to strike out on their own as a pattern designer?

You need to really find your own style and practice like mad. You have to be a little bit obsessive about it. Also, be prepared for knockbacks when you submit your work but don't take that as a sign that you should stop, take it as a sign that you should keep going because it doesn't mean that your work isn't any good, it just means that it's perhaps not what a buyer is looking for at that particular moment or maybe you're targeting the wrong companies for your work. I recently landed a licencing deal that took about two years to be confirmed and so sometimes it just requires patience. Doing research can also help with finding out where your work would fit best. Look at stores you like and see what products they are selling.

What is your favourite colour combination?

I really don't have a favourite, but I'm definitely drawn to brights and I do love slightly discordant colours that are quirky and create a little element of surprise.

surroundings, nature, family, everyday objects and simple pleasures.

Do you have a favourite client collaboration in your career so far?

I'm still pretty new to the licencing world, but of the work I have done so far I think my favourite would be working with Midwest-CBK on my gift and homeware range.

How has working with an artist agent changed the way you approach designing new patterns?

Working with my agent, Lilla Rogers, has been such a positive experience for me and I'm so grateful and happy to be one of her artists. She is so giving and continually shares her trend reports with us and gives us lovely inspiration to work from. Her classes also really helped me to take that jump forward with my artwork. I now have a much clearer view on what I need to do when I create new work. I have also learned that you don't really need to know how to do a technical repeat to have your work on a fabric line, you just have to produce beautiful, eye-catching art.

GIFT WRAP GALLERY

Above: Lithograph-printed Recycled Geometric wrapping paper by MULK. Photo by Ryan Mason Images. **Left:** Totem gift wrap by Lucie Summers, Summersville. Photo by Lucie Summers. **Below:** Hand-printed gift wrap by Mariam Eqbal. Photo by Mariam Eqbal.

Left: Watercolour Citrus Fruits gift wrap paper by Pineapple bay studio. Photo by Susan Magdangal. **Below:** Follow the Arrow gift wrap by Toodles Noodles. Photo by Eleanor at JEL.
Bottom: Hammerpress gift wrap. Photo by Hammerpress.
[All images on this page are copyright to the producers and photographers. They are for inspiration only, and not for use in commercial projects.]

Chapter Seven
STATIONERY

If you are anything like me, greeting cards, journals, gift tags and anything else stationery-related are a never-ending visual delight. I love shopping for paper goods and will never tire of the beautiful colours, the feel of the paper, the infinite design options . . . I don't think the art of the hand-written note or the diary will ever die completely as long as beautiful stationery exists in the world!

In this age of email, social media and computers galore, it feels mandatory and vital to me that we step away from our devices from time to time to create simple, beautiful objects with our hands. Printing your own stationery is simple, fun and extremely satisfying. The printing process is relatively quick on these smaller paper products, so you can create a lot in a short amount of time.

Rubber block stamping is my favourite technique to use on paper, but experiment with the other printing methods used throughout the book, such as potato stamping, screen printing and stencilling, to discover which you like the best.

Hand-printed greeting card by Jessica Swift. Photo by Jessica Nichols.

APPLYING PATTERNS TO NOTEBOOKS AND CARDS

These tutorials will teach you how to use rubber block stamps to create your own hand-printed notebooks, cards, and coordinating envelopes. Rubber block printing is a wonderful technique for printing your own stationery as it's a fun and easy process that yields quick results.

When printing on small, flat surfaces like cards and envelopes, scrap paper will be your best friend. I am somewhat of a messy printer and I tend to get ink all over the place. Scrap paper helps me to insure that I don't drag my project through some stray wet ink and ruin it. Placing a sheet of scrap paper underneath any edge of your project that you may need to print over to finish a row will help you protect both your project and your printing surface from ink. Be careful not to shift your card, envelope, notebook or paper too much as you print to avoid getting stray ink on the back of your project.

Doing a test print before printing on your final object can help you avoid mistakes. Experiment with the amount of ink to roll onto your stamp and the amount of pressure you'll need to apply to it by printing onto a scrap sheet of paper or an extra card, envelope or notebook.

Your stationery projects can be as simple or as complicated as you'd like. As you become more comfortable using rubber block stamps, you can vary your techniques and materials and create truly unique projects. The tutorials use simple blank cards, envelopes and notebooks in a variety of colours.

IDEAS ON TAKING YOUR HAND-PRINTING TO THE NEXT LEVEL

- Stamp large sheets of card and cut them down to card or gift tag size.
- Use a sewing machine to sew together different strips of hand-printed paper to create unique cards.
- Fold your own interesting envelopes out of your printed paper.
- Print on thick card and use as a cover to create your own handmade notebooks.
- Paint washes of colour on a large sheet of watercolour paper and use as a background on which to print. Cut down to card, gift tag or notebook cover size.

Hand-printed stationery by Jessica Swift. Photos by Jessica Nichols.

STAMPING CARDS AND ENVELOPES

Step 1

Secure your blank card with masking tape on a sheet of scrap paper on top of a flat surface. Squeeze ink onto your palette and roll your brayer through it until it's coated evenly with a thin layer of ink. Roll the brayer over the surface of your stamp, coating it evenly with a thin layer of ink.

Step 2

Starting at the bottom left of the card, place stamp face down and press firmly for several seconds. Lift the stamp.

Step 3

To create a straight repeat, repeat step 2 to finish the bottom row. Stamp over the edges of the card onto the scrap paper if needed to finish the row. Start the next row directly above the first.

Step 4

Repeat steps 3 and 4 until you've reached the top of the card. Set the card aside to dry. Rinse and dry your brayer and stamp.

Step 5

To create a co-ordinating design and to leave room on the envelope to write an address, choose one area of the envelope that you will stamp. Stamp as in steps 3 and 4 until the area is complete.

SEE ALSO Scale and spacing, p. 43; Rubber block stamps, p. 56

WHAT YOU'LL NEED

- Blank card and co-ordinating envelope
- Several sheets of scrap paper
- Masking tape
- Block-printing ink
- Palette for ink (wax paper or a sheet of clear acrylic)
- Brayer
- Carved rubber block stamp or foam stamp (see pp. 56-58)

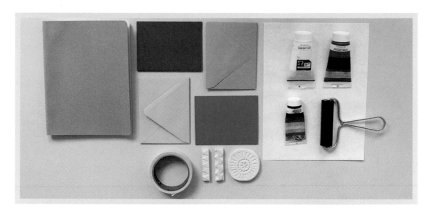

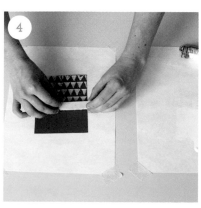

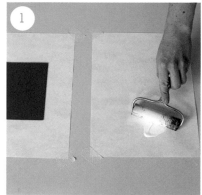

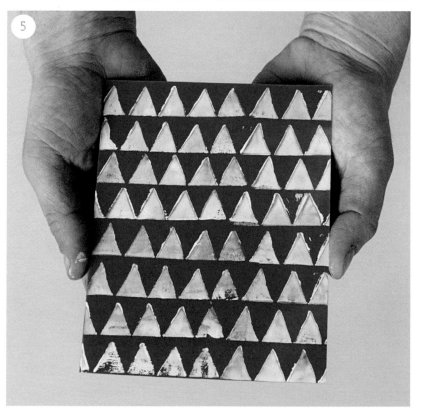

PRINTING ON A NOTEBOOK

Step 1

Lay your notebook on a flat surface. Place a sheet of scrap paper underneath the notebook cover to protect your surface from any ink when printing over the edges. Squeeze the first ink colour onto your palette and roll your brayer through the ink until it's coated evenly. Roll the brayer over the surface of your stamp, coating it evenly.

Step 2

Starting anywhere in the centre of the notebook, place stamp face down and press firmly for several seconds. Lift the stamp.

Step 3

Repeat step 2, stamping in a random pattern to create a tossed repeat and spacing widely to leave room for the second stamp. When finished, rinse and dry your stamp and brayer.

Step 4

Squeeze the second ink colour onto your palette and roll your brayer through the ink until it's coated evenly with a thin layer. Roll the brayer over the surface of your second stamp, coating it evenly. Starting in any blank space on the notebook, place stamp face down and press firmly for several seconds. Lift the stamp. Repeat until all blank areas are filled to your liking.

Step 5

Using the eraser end of a pencil (or any other dot-making tool), stamp dots in random spaces as an accent.

Step 6

Leave to dry. Repeat steps 1 to 5 on the back cover of the notebook.

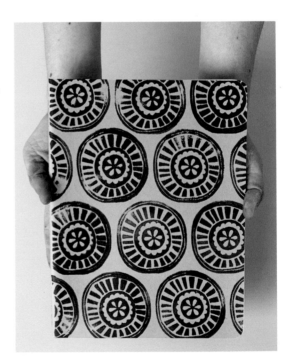

SEE ALSO Choosing colours, p. 24; Motif styles, p. 30

USING PATTERNS

WHAT YOU'LL NEED

- Journal with a blank cover
- Block-printing ink (2-3 colours)
- Palette for ink (wax paper)
- Brayer
- 2 carved rubber block stamps (see p. 56)
- Several sheets of scrap paper
- Eraser-tipped pencil for dots

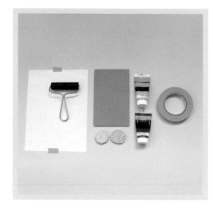

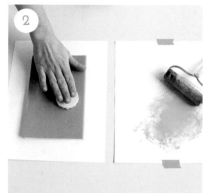

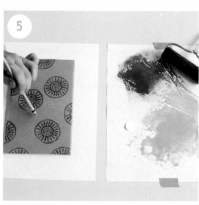

Interview
LEAH DUNCAN

PROFESSION: Pattern designer
COUNTRY: United States of America

Your colour sensibility is very unique and beautiful. Where do you find your colour inspiration?

I love soft colours with a slight organic feel. I never studied colour theory or went to art college, so I think my colour palette comes from an innate sensibility that's always been tucked away. If given acrylic paint, crayons, or the palette swatches in a design program, I'll always mix the same colours without any intention of doing so. I work with colour until it

feels just right. Because I'm from the South there's influence from the Victorian colour schemes that dot the architecture of Southeastern America. Now that I live in Texas things have gotten much sunnier with warmer colour palettes, wildflowers and south-western themes influencing my work.

What is your creative process like? Do you plan a new design, or do you work more intuitively?

It normally starts with an idea,

but it almost never ends up as I intended. I work more intuitively and am constantly changing direction as I go. I like to think of the creative process as a journey, not a blueprint. It can at times be frustrating and a little hard to break through, but the end is always better than anything I could have initially planned.

How has your work changed and evolved since you first started designing patterns?

I fell in love with pattern while

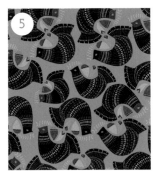

working as a graphic designer after college. I loved the thought of repetition, the way elements play off of each other and how an object can be duplicated over and over to create something completely new. Obviously my ability has grown, but I've also matured a lot as a person and an artist since then. I'm a kid at heart, so there will always be room for whimsical themes in my life, but I've recently felt a need to simplify while also making aspects of my work more sophisticated. It's interesting to see how my intention, inspiration and body of work has evolved. Only time will tell where this journey takes me.

Where do you find inspiration for the quirky and original motifs in your work?

I'm a rather quirky person deep down with a lot of strange habits, so I think the quirkiness in my work is simply a direct reflection of who I am. As for motifs, I'm mostly influenced by environments and small moments in my life. I love nature and animals, so those themes often sneak in. For me, it's always been about communicating, sharing and translating moments in a simple and beautiful way. I'm not even sure how to describe inspiration. As artists I think we're constantly soaking in ideas, themes and influence everywhere we go. The 'art' part of it is the translation. It's how we filter those ideas into our own work to make something unique.

What advice can you give to someone who wants to design their own patterned products?

It is very worthwhile to work hard to have a distinctive body of work. The more people recognise your work the more they will remember it and the more they remember it, the more they'll be prompted to return to it.

What is your favourite colour combination?

Ochre, peachy pink and indigo. It's so feminine yet bold and earthy. It reminds me of the desert.

1: Mountains pattern by Leah Duncan;
2: Place mats made with Meadow Fabric Collection by Leah Duncan. Photo by Art Gallery Fabrics;
3: Pillow covers made with Meadow Fabric Collection by Leah Duncan. Photo by Art Gallery Fabrics;
4: Elena Tribal pattern by Leah Duncan;
5: Hens pattern by Leah Duncan.

STATIONERY GALLERY

Above: Hive notecard set by Wit & Whistle. Photo by Amanda Wright. **Left:** Linoleum block-printed notecard by Katharine Watson. Photo by Katharine Watson. **Below:** Matryoshka journal by Jessica Swift for teNeues Publishing. Photo by Jessica Swift.

Left: Rock the Casbah GreenBooklets by Ampersand Design Studio for teNeues Publishing. Photo by Ampersand Design Studio.
Below: Smooshi Calendar by Smooshi. Photo by EsteStudio.
Bottom: Smooshi Calendar by Smooshi. Photo by EsteStudio.
[All images on this page are copyright to the producers and photographers. They are for inspiration only, and not for use in commercial projects.]

Chapter Eight
PACKAGING

Whether you want to add a unique touch to your product packaging or you want to learn some fun new techniques for creating beautifully packaged gifts, putting your own handmade patterns on boxes, bags and tags will help you add a new dimension and personal detail to your packaging endeavours.

I love boxes and have spent many a day in my life creating special containers using collaging, photo transfers, drawing, colouring and hand-printing, in which to keep bits and bobs. Blank wooden and cardboard boxes and blank paper bags in all colours are easy to purchase at craft, art, and often party stores, as well as online; they are affordable blank canvases on which to create your own beautiful designs.

I never tire of seeing all the hand-printed goodies I've created all piled together in a glorious mash-up of colours and patterns, and if you're anything like me you'll find these techniques wonderfully addictive and will become obsessed with creating beautiful piles of beautifully hand-printed packaging pieces all your own!

Hand-printed gift bags by Jessica Swift. Photo by Jessica Nichols.

APPLYING PATTERNS TO BOXES AND BAGS

The three-dimensionality of boxes and bags make them perfect surfaces for showcasing hand-printed patterns in interesting ways. Paper, glassine, wood, cardboard, plastic – try printing on all of them and see what sorts of beautiful and unique creations you can conjure!

These tutorials will teach you how to use a potato stamp to create hand-printed patterns on adorable little boxes, and you'll also learn to stencil a pattern onto paper gift bags. As with all the techniques in this book, these are only suggestions. You could just as easily use a hand-carved rubber stamp or a stencil to print onto boxes, a screen print or a foam stamp to print onto bags, and any other combinations you'd like to try.

When using stencils, there are some options for inking techniques. You can use a foam roller to lay on your colour to achieve a coat of flat, thin paint. Spray paint also works well. You can also try using a stencil brush, which is a paintbrush made of thick bristles with a flat, round top. Stencil brushes come in a variety of sizes.

In addition to experimenting with ways of applying the patterns, you can experiment with different pattern layouts as well. Single motifs are very versatile – you could turn the same potato stamp into a straight repeat, a half-drop repeat, a brick repeat or a tossed repeat. You could combine multiple motifs (stamps, stencils or otherwise) to create a more complex pattern based on the very same types of repeats. Adding in more variety will always make a pattern appear more complex. Remember, more is not always better! Sometimes a beautiful, bold, graphic, single-motif pattern is more striking than one that's overly busy with lots of different shapes and colours.

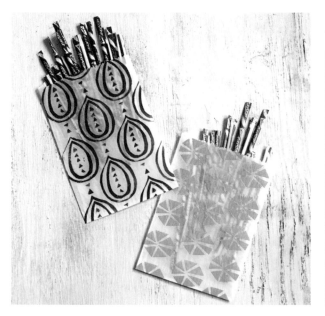

Hand-printed boxes and bags by Jessica Swift. Photos by Jessica Nichols.

Tutorial
POTATO STAMPING A BOX

BEFORE YOU BEGIN

You'll need to make your potato stamps. For this project you will need one small and one large. Cut a potato in half with a kitchen knife. On the flat surface of one of the potato halves, draw a motif with a pen, or start carving a motif freehand. Remember to think about which areas will be carved away and which will remain uncarved. To begin, use very light pressure on your carving tool or craft knife, to carve away the areas that will be negative space. Deepen your cuts once you've established your shapes. Rinse your potato under running water to remove any extra bits of potato carving, and then dry.

Step 1

Set your box on a flat surface with a sheet of scrap paper underneath. Squeeze ink onto your palette and roll your brayer through it until it's coated evenly. Roll the brayer over the surface of your larger potato stamp, coating it evenly with a thin layer of ink.

Step 2

Choose a starting place on your box, and place inked stamp face down. Press firmly for several seconds. Lift the stamp.

Step 3

Leave space between prints, so you can use the smaller stamp later to print in the empty spaces. Continue inking your stamp and printing in a random, tossed repeat pattern on all exterior faces, except the base, of your box and its lid.

Step 4

Rinse your brayer and potato stamp. Dry the brayer completely, squeeze out your second colour of ink onto your palette, and ink your brayer and smaller potato stamp as in step 1.

Step 5

Being careful not to smear your first layer of prints, use your smaller inked stamp to fill in some of the blank areas you left in step 3. Continue inking your stamp and printing until you've filled all the open areas to create a lovely tossed pattern.

Step 6

Let the box and lid dry completely before using it.

TOP TIP

Keep your potato stamp in a bowl of water in the refrigerator when you're not using it to make it last longer.

SEE ALSO Direction and orientation, p. 42; Designing a motif, p. 46

WHAT YOU'LL NEED

- 2 carved potato stamps (see box opposite), one larger and one smaller
- Several sheets of scrap paper
- Block-printing ink (2 colours)
- Palette for ink (wax paper or sheet of clear acrylic)
- Brayer
- Blank box (cardboard, paper or wood)

STENCILLING ON A PAPER BAG

BEFORE YOU BEGIN

Stencilling onto the folding sides of bags can be tricky; if your bag has folded sides and you want to print on them, try cutting a piece of firm cardboard to place inside the bag to keep the folded edge flat or insert a block or box of some kind inside the bag to hold the folded edge in place. Stencil using the method above, or alternatively, use a different printing method (rubber block print, pencil eraser print, spray painting through a stencil or doily, for example) to create a complementary pattern on the sides of the bag.

Step 1

Set a blank paper bag on a flat surface, laying scrap paper underneath to catch stray ink. Squeeze paint onto your palette and roll your foam roller through it until it's coated evenly with a thin layer of paint.

Step 2

Place your stencil on the bag, starting in the bottom left corner. Hold down firmly, so the stencil and the bag are in full contact. (The closer the contact between the two surfaces, the crisper the stenciled print.) Roll the foam roller lightly over the surface of the stencil, making sure the paint fills all areas of the stencil. Be careful not to roll beyond the edges of the stencil, so you don't create any unwanted paint markings.

Step 3

Lift the stencil and move it up so the bottom edge of the stencil is just above the top of your first print. Repeat step 2 to create your second print and continue printing up the bag to finish your first row. (If you're using a stencil brush, dab paint onto the stencil, holding your brush perpendicular to the printing surface, until all areas of the stencil are filled with a thin layer of paint.)

Step 4

When the first column is dry, place your stencil midway between the first and second prints at the bottom of the first column. This will create a half-drop repeat. Repeat steps 2 and 3 to finish the second column. If you need to print over the edges of the bag to finish a column, place a sheet of scrap paper underneath to protect your printing surface from wet paint.

Step 5

Repeat steps 2 to 4 to finish printing the entire surface, and then repeat all steps to stencil the back of the bag.

SEE ALSO Scale and spacing, p. 43; Stencils, p. 60

WHAT YOU'LL NEED

- Pre-cut stencil (see p. 60)
- Several sheets of scrap paper
- Blank paper bag (any size, shape or colour)
- Craft paint
- Palette for paint (wax paper or sheet of acrylic)
- Small foam roller or stencil brush
- Masking tape (to secure your stencil)
- Rag or paper towels (to clean unwanted excess paint from your stencil)

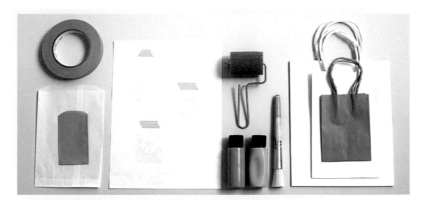

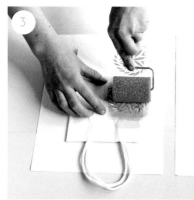

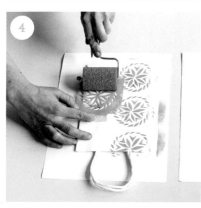

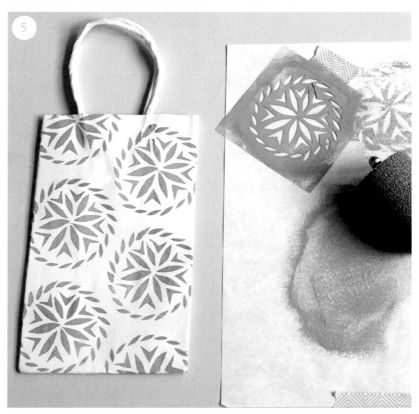

SUSANNE FIRMENICH (HAMBURGER LIEBE)

PROFESSION: Pattern and textile designer
COUNTRY: Germany

When and how did you come to be a pattern designer?

That happened totally unexpectedly. About six years ago I started writing a blog, Hamburger Liebe. I wanted to share my DIY projects and the things I was sewing for my children. After I showed some illustrations for melamine plates that I scribbled for my two little nieces, I got a request to develop designs for machine embroidery files. Another company then asked for designs for woven ribbons. This was my entry into textile design. During my research for pretty fabrics (which were hard to find), I discovered an online print-on-demand service for fabrics.

You can upload your own designs and have them printed on different types of fabric. I was thrilled with this new opportunity and shared the results on my blog. A short time after my debut on a newly created digital marketplace I got my first request to produce fabric designs on a regular basis. I now truly was smitten with textile design. I quit my job as a freelance graphic designer to become a textile designer. It was not always easy and it demanded a lot of patience. I have been collaborating for over two years with a company - Hilco - who produce and distribute my designs.

1: Chevron quilt, Happy Fabric Collection;
2: My Aunties and An Apple A Day Woven Ribbon Collections;
3: Union Jack cushion, Happy Fabric Collection,
all by Hamburger Liebe. Photos by Susan Firmenich.

How have your years as a graphic designer influenced your pattern design and your brand identity?

I gathered great experiences in working for brands over the years and these have been very helpful in building my own brand now. What I learned, and what frustrated me most, was the fact that everything in graphic design is ephemeral. The things you create are outdated one day after their release. Your work is thrown away, no matter how passionately it was created, but I wanted to create something that lasts. I didn't use my illustration talent much during my time as a graphic designer, it was more like a hobby. I had always dreamed of illustrating children's books. I started doing a whole new thing when I began working as a textile designer. It was so exciting and still is!

The photographs on your blog, Hamburger Liebe, are gorgeous! Has product photography been important for you in creating such a vibrant, successful business?

Thank you so much! I think that representing your product/creation with good and professional-looking pictures is essential for your success. It starts with the presentation – no one wants to see the mess in your studio – and ends with a sharp and well-lit picture. Therefore you don't need any expensive camera equipment – I didn't and still don't. Top tip: daylight is your friend!

Your colours and motifs are beautiful – both playful and sophisticated all at once. Where do you find inspiration?

I find inspiration everywhere I go! I'm a visual person. I soak up everything I see. Lights, colours, nice packages in the super-market, patterns on walls, and things my kids create. When I have an idea, I scribble on anything that I have on me: receipts, slips of paper, newspapers. I also love my Pantone Colour Guide. I could sit for hours and match colours.

What is your favourite colour combination?

You know that I love colours! I definitely can't reduce it to a handful. They change every day! But right now I would say my favourite combination is ruby-tangerine-hot pink-mint. Or no, wait . . .

What advice can you give someone who wants to build a recognisable brand image?

That is hard to say in a few words. Be unique, find out what your talent is, and concentrate on one target. Don't compare yourself to others and do your business with passion. Everything without passion will fail.

PACKAGING GALLERY

Above: Deco Collection Shea Butter Soap by The Soap and Paper Factory. Photo by Angel Tucker. **Left:** Deco Collection Shea Butter Soap by The Soap and Paper Factory. Photo by Angel Tucker. **Below:** TeaPee by Sophie Pépin. Photo by Sophie Pépin.

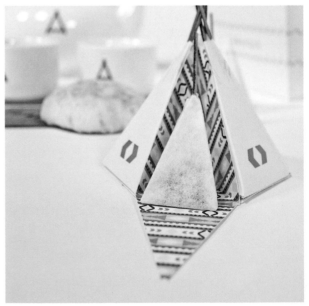

Top: Pasta packaging by Alessia Olivari. Photo by Alessia Olivari. **Bottom:** Decorative match boxes by BelloPop. Photo by Andreina Bello. [All images on this page are copyright to the producers and photographers. They are for inspiration only, and not for use in commercial projects.]

Chapter Nine
IN THE HOME

On a trip to visit my family in Colorado a couple of years ago, I walked into the entryway of my mum's house and stepped onto a fantastic tiled floor. She excitedly told me that while she was out searching for treasures in a charity shop one day, she found a cool decorative stamp that she thought might be the exact size and shape of the tiles on her floor. She'd been looking for a way to spruce up the space, and she instantly thought of stamping on the tiles. She hurried home to try it out and, lo and behold, it was a perfect fit! The result was a stunning floor that was amazingly quick and easy to create.

Applying patterns to your home doesn't need to be expensive or difficult. There's no need to buy rolls of pricey wallpaper or instal a new floor - applying hand-printed patterns to what you've already got is a fun and easy way to change the look and feel of your home and add a personal and completely unique touch. The techniques here are not limited to use on walls and tile floors either: furniture, frames, rugs, cement floors, pillows and shower curtains are just a few of the other types of surfaces that are perfect for hand-printing projects. Now, go fill your home with patterns!

Hand-printed tiles by Jessica Swift. Photo by Jessica Nichols.

APPLYING PATTERNS TO WALLS AND FLOORS

From visualising the pattern tile as a series of ceramic tiles to printing on actual ceramic tiles using a multi-motif rubber block stamp, you've come a long way! If you've ever admired beautiful patterned tiles before, you're going to love making your own!

Printing a pattern on a floor need not be confined to tiled floors – why not try printing on a wood or cement floor? Start by creating a design that works as a straight repeat using multiple motifs on paper, turn that design into a stamp or a stencil and then print the design in rows directly on the floor. Using the same stamp or stencil, you can vary the technique by leaving a bit of space between each print for an easy faux-tiled look. The walls in your home are just another blank canvas for patterns. Make a stencil and paint a bold, graphic border pattern onto a wall. There is plenty of room for experimentation with this technique. It's easy turn a border pattern into a design for an entire wall by simply stencilling multiple rows below one another. Or, you could stencil along the top edge of a wooden fence to make your outdoor space a little more cheery, or stencil a design onto an old wooden table. Get creative and you'll begin to notice all the interesting places available for applying a bit of pattern in your home.

Clear adhesive shelf-liner is a fun alternative for making stencils. These stencils won't last as long as those made from acetate, but the adhesive backing is useful for tight adhesion to the surface making for crisp, clear stencil lines. The downside with a contact paper stencil is that repeated sticking and peeling will damage the stencil and reduce adhesion, so this material is best used on a small project with few repeats. The cautious crafter, though, could make multiple versions of their master stencil.

Left: Gingko Leaf rug by Jessica Swift for Chandra Rugs. Photo by Ryan Gibson. Opposite page, top: Throws by Happy Habitat. Photo by Karrie Kaneda; Bottom: Lotus rugs by Jessica Swift for Chandra Rugs. Photo by Ryan Gibson.

STENCILLING A BORDER ON A WALL

Step 1

Figure out how far from the edge of the wall you'd like to stencil your design. The simplest way is to line up the edge of the stencil with the edge of the wall. Starting at the top of the wall, place your stencil flat and secure it on the wall with masking tape. You could use the same method for a vertical design but line up your stencil from the floor or where the wall meets the ceiling.

Step 2

Squeeze some paint onto your palette. Coat your paintbrush or foam roller with a thin coat of paint.

Step 3

Carefully and lightly dab the paintbrush into the cut areas of the stencil. If using a roller, roll it over the stencil to fill the cut areas with a thick, even coat of paint. Leave to dry for several minutes.

Step 4

Carefully remove stencil from the wall. If necessary, clean any paint off the back of the stencil. Reposition the stencil directly below and in line with the first print to create a straight repeat. Secure around the edges with masking tape.

Step 5

Repeat steps 2 to 4 until you reach the bottom of the wall. The bottom-most stencil print may end up being a partial design, depending on the size of your stencil and the length of the wall. Repeat steps 2 to 5 on any other edges or areas of wall (for example, if you're stencilling around a door or window) you'd like to stencil.

SEE ALSO Building a colour palette, p. 26; Stencils, p. 60

WHAT YOU'LL NEED

- Pre-cut stencil (see p. 60)
- Blank wall area
- Masking tape
- Stencil brush or small foam roller
- Acrylic or craft paint
- Palette for paint (wax paper or sheet of acrylic)

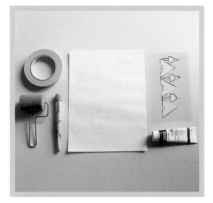

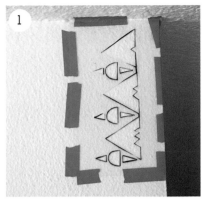

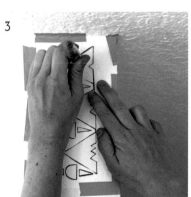

Tutorial
PRINTING ON TILES

The tiles in this tutorial are 5 x 5 centimetres (2 x 2 in), but any size tile will work. Just make sure your carved stamp is the same size as your tile or that it's a multiple of the tile's height and width. (For example, you could use a 5 x 5-centimetre (2 x 2-in) carved stamp on a 10 x 10-centimetre (4 x 4-in) tile by stamping four times on each tile or on a 10 x 20-centimetre (4 x 8-in) tile by stamping eight times per tile and the pattern would repeat properly, but if you used a 5 x 5-centimetre (2 x 2-in) stamp on a 10 x 23-centimetre (4 x 9-in) tile the repeat would not work).

BEFORE YOU BEGIN

To carve a multi-motif rubber stamp that will repeat properly, use the tutorials on pages 48–56 to create your pattern tile on paper, and then use the tutorial on page 56, which shows how to transfer the design onto a rubber block and how to carve your design to create the stamp. In this tutorial we have used a complex straight repeat, but you can use whatever pattern you like.

Step 1

Lay a blank ceramic tile on a sheet of scrap paper on a flat surface. Squeeze ink onto your palette and roll your brayer through it until it's coated evenly with a thin layer of ink. Roll the brayer over the surface of your stamp, coating it evenly with ink.

Step 2

Place the stamp surface over the tile, taking care to make sure it is lined up squarely. Gently press the stamp onto the tile, being careful not to shift its placement. Lift the stamp.

Step 3

Repeat steps 1 and 2 on each tile, positioning the stamp in the same direction for each print. Leave the tiles to dry overnight.

Step 4

Spray with four to five coats of clear gloss spray and leave to dry. Brush on at least three coats of polyurethane to seal the ink. Leave the tiles to dry overnight.

Step 5

When the tiles have dried, rub a damp cloth over one tile to test how well the ink is sealed. If necessary, apply more coats of polyurethane. When fully dry, the tiles are ready for use.

▼

SEE ALSO Layout and symmetry, p. 40; Rubber block stamps, p. 56

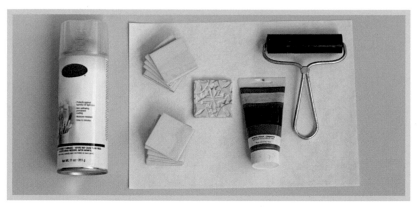

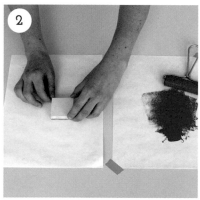

WHAT YOU'LL NEED

- Ceramic tiles
- Carved rubber block stamp, same dimensions as your ceramic tiles
- Several sheets of scrap paper
- Block-printing ink
- Palette for ink (wax paper or a sheet of acrylic)
- Brayer
- Clear gloss spray finish
- Can of polyurethane
- Soft cloth

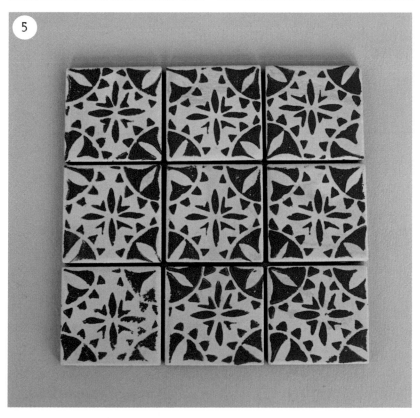

HEATHER MOORE (SKINNY LAMINX)

PROFESSION: Fabric designer
COUNTRY: South Africa

Your process of turning paper cuts into fabric designs is quite unique. How did you develop this way of working?

When I first started working on fabric, I had just one silk screen frame and no experience with the technique, so I started cutting out stencils just to give screen printing a bash. I used paper and occasionally sticky vinyl, and I enjoyed the cutting process a lot. Of course the cut outs got destroyed after a few pulls on the screen, so I learned to keep

those ones quite simple. I started doing more complicated cut outs that I then had exposed onto screens so that I could get better use out of all that hard work!

Where do you find inspiration for the motifs and colours you use?

I've always found the motifs and colours of design from the mid-twentieth century quite inspiring. So those muddy yellows and dirty blues, greys and pinks all formed part of my early palette. As far as motifs

go, I keep a sketchbook and I take a lot of photos, and this recording process seems to put me onto a track that develops into a print or a collection. Right now, my eye is very tuned to seeing plants in a city context.

Do you have a favourite product that has been made using one of your fabric designs?

I think that my Flower Fields design, in Penny Black, is currently my favourite. We're about to launch some of our

prints on wallpaper, and I'm particularly excited about seeing this design - slightly scaled up - on a wall!

What are some of the challenges that come along with designing patterns to be screen-printed onto fabric?

One of the major challenges is cost, as each colour in a design requires a rather pricey screen of its own. Also, each colour adds more risk to the production, as it takes a number of passes to complete the design. Luckily, I tend to like very simple, flat designs. Screen printing flat colours requires expertise too, as pressure needs to be even in order for the colour to come out clear and even. Then there's also the issue of registration in multi-colour design, which needs to be carefully designed around.

What tips can you share about how to begin screen printing your own fabric?

I started screenprinting with just one screen, a squeegee and a cutting knife. I would experiment with cutting stencils from paper, acetate, sticky vinyl and lots more, and although I made a lot of rubbish prints, I got an idea about the principles behind the technique, which helped me to make better designs. If you don't have a screen, you can try stretching a fine mesh fabric across an embroidery hoop and use a credit card as a squeegee. It works surprisingly well!

What is your favourite colour combination?

Oh, this is a difficult question, and the answer keeps changing! One of the things I really enjoy about having a store is that now and again, a customer will come in and assemble a colour combination that would never have occurred to me.

1: Screen-printed fabric, Rough Cuts Collection;
2: Acid Pastels cushions and totes;
3: Mushrooms apron;
4: Soft fabric bucket in Inkspot colourway, all by Skinny laMinx. Photos by Heather Moore.

IN THE HOME GALLERY

Above: Hundreds and Thousands condiment tray by Jonna Saarinen. Photo by Jonna Saarinen. **Left:** Small Kilim bench by Barrington Blue. Photo by Carrie Olshan. **Below:** Bloomsbury bone china by Lucie Summers, Summersville. Photo by Lucie Summers.

Chapter Ten

RESOURCES

To get you started in your pattern design adventures, I've included 20 copyright-free motifs here for you to use in your own projects. You can change or adapt as you please. You can trace them, photocopy them, cut them out, scan them into your computer, use them in combination with your own motifs or on their own – whatever you like. I hope they're helpful and inspiring as you begin to create your own beautiful patterns.

Please remember to be careful when you are using images for inspiration. If you choose to use images and motifs that are not your own, they must be absolutely free of any copyright. If you are not sure, don't use them. The motifs on the following two pages are copyright-free and are available for you to use as you please, but remember the rest of the images in this book (both my own images and those on the interview and gallery pages) are copyrighted images and are to inspire you – they are not available for use in any way in your own designs.

A number of resources are included on the following pages for image and colour inspiration as well as online courses, blogs and websites where you can learn more about pattern design. If you are ready to take your pattern designs to the next level – from hand-printed products to ones that are printed digitally onto other items – I've included a list of some website platforms which make that possible for independent artists and crafters. We live in an exciting time as artists, and the Internet gives us the capability to create products that we could only have dreamed of in years past.

I hope you'll fall in love with pattern design the way that I have, and that this book and the resources listed here serve as stepping stones along your creative path. It's a never-endingly delightful road, and I wish you all my very, most colourful best along the way!

Hand-carved and handmade stamps by Jessica Swift. Photo by Jessica Nichols.

MOTIF TEMPLATES

These motif templates are easy to download, resize and print. You can photocopy them, resizing according to your needs, or simply scan the corresponding QR codes or type in the weblink and download.

1   http://bit.ly/1BVWW86

2   http://bit.ly/1CXzYQk

3   http://bit.ly/1uFm8Q3

4   http://bit.ly/1vTe26R

5   http://bit.ly/1qocjzV

6   http://bit.ly/1ne3bmt

7   http://bit.ly/1BW11JD

8   http://bit.ly/1qoelQv

9   http://bit.ly/1uFoGhh

http://bit.ly/1EyfX4A

http://bit.ly/1vTgbiV

http://bit.ly/1v6bsLV

http://bit.ly/1vTgPgh

http://bit.ly/1vQGmVA

http://bit.ly/1EyitYP

http://bit.ly/1ybOYvT

http://bit.ly/1oTVJZc

http://bit.ly/1oTW3ar

http://bit.ly/1sfoeW6

http://bit.ly/ZtXnKw

PRINTING AND IMAGE RESOURCES

PRINTING

Custom Printed Gift Wrap
www.customgiftwrap.co.uk

Design Your Wall
www.designyourwall.com/store/
favouritedrawing.php

Envelop
www.envelop.eu

Fabric On Demand
www.fabricondemand.com

Society 6
www.society6.com

Spoonflower
www.spoonflower.com

Stationery HQ
www.stationeryhq.com/
wrapping-paper

IMAGES

Clipart.com
www.clipart.com

Dover Online Clip Art Store
www.store.doverpublications.
com/by-subject-clip-art.html

Dover Pictura
www.doverpictura.com

Dover Publications
www.doverpublications.com

The Graphics Fairy
www.thegraphicsfairy.com

Public Domain Clip Art
www.pdclipart.org

Schiffer Books
www.schifferbooks.com

Shutterstock
www.shutterstock.com

ThinkStock
www.thinkstockphotos.com

Vectorportal
www.vectorportal.com

VectorStock
www.vectorstock.com

Vintage Printable
www.vintageprintable.com

USEFUL WEBSITES AND COMPANIES

COLOUR
COLOURLovers
www.colourlovers.com
Design Seeds
www.design-seeds.com
Pantone
www.pantone.com

BLOGS AND PUBLICATIONS
Moyo Magazine
www.makeitindesign.com/
moyo-magazine
Pantone blog
www.blog.pantone.com
Pattern Observer
www.patternobserver.com
Pattern People
www.patternpeople.com
Print & Pattern
www.printpattern.blogspot.com
Tigerprint
www.designcompetition.
tigerprint.uk.com

DESIGN COURSES AND TUTORIALS
Creative Live
www.creativelive.com
Instructables
www.instructables.com
Make It In Design
www.makeitindesign.com/
design-school
Nicole's Classes
www.nicolesclasses.com
Pattern Observer
www.patternobserver.com/
courses
Skillshare
www.skillshare.com

E-COMMERCE PLATFORMS
Envelop
www.envelop.eu
Etsy
www.etsy.com
Folksy
www.folksy.com

Society 6
www.society6.com
Spoonflower
www.spoonflower.com

SUPPLIES
B&H Photo, Video, Pro Audio
www.bhphotovideo.com
(for the Cyanotype printing kit,
see Cyanotype printing on
paper, p. 88).
Blick Art Supplies
www.dickblick.com
Cutting Edge Stencils
www.cuttingedgestencils.com
Michaels
www.michaels.com
Paper Source
www.papersource.com
Royal Design Studio Stencils
www.royaldesignstudio.com
Standard Screen Supply Corp
www.standardscreen.com

Left: Triangles wallpaper by Lisa Congdon for Hygge & West. Photo by Hygge & West. **Below:** Elephant Love Fabric Collection by Susanne Firmenich, Hamburger Liebe. Photo by Susanne Firmenich.

GLOSSARY

Acetate
A sheet of thin plastic that can be used to make stencils.

Acrylic plastic
A sheet of plastic, often transparent like glass, that is useful as a reusable palette for paint and ink.

Allover repeat
A pattern where the motifs are close together, so little to no background is showing.

Analogous colours
These are colours that are next to one another on the colour wheel (for example: red, orange and yellow).

Block printing
A technique where a carved material (often wood, rubber or linoleum) is pressed onto a printing surface (usually paper or fabric), by hand or with a printing press to leave a raised ink print.

Block repeat
A type of pattern repeat where the underlying structure of the repeating units is a grid-like formation. (See also Square repeat and Straight repeat.)

Brayer
A small, smooth hand-held roller used to apply a thin and even coat of ink to the surface of a stamp.

Brick repeat
A type of pattern repeat where the repeating units are staggered horizontally in a brick-like layout.

Carbon transfer paper
A type of paper coated with carbon on one side, used as a tracing medium to transfer a design from paper to another surface.

Clamshell repeat
A type of pattern layout where overlapping arcs or circles create a scale-like repeating pattern.

Clear acrylic
A type of thin, flat acrylic plastic, often transparent like glass and available in sheets, that is useful as a reusable palette for paint and ink.

Complementary colour
These are colours that are directly across from one another on the colour wheel (for example: blue and orange).

Conversational prints
A style of pattern where all or some of the motifs are recognisable objects. (Also called Novelty prints or Object prints.)

Diamond repeat
A type of pattern layout where the typical underlying grid of squares or rectangles is rotated 45° to create a grid of diamonds.

Directional pattern
A type of pattern repeat that is meant to be viewed in either one direction or two. It is common for novelty prints to be directional patterns because of the recognisable nature of the motifs. (Also called One-way and Two-way patterns.)

Foam printing
A technique used for hand printing in which a stamp is made by adhering a motif cut from a flat, thin sheet of foam to an acrylic or wood block.

Four-way pattern
A type of repeat that can be viewed in four directions. Motifs are generally laid out in a geometric way in four directions so the pattern looks the same when rotated 90°. (See also Non-directional pattern.)

Furoshiki
A Japanese wrapping cloth, used to wrap gifts, made from a square fabric that is often patterned.

Geometric pattern
A style of pattern where the motifs are non representational, such as circles, squares, lines and dots.

Half-drop repeat
A type of pattern layout where every other column of motifs is staggered vertically half way down the length of the repeating units.

Hexagon repeat
A pattern layout where the underlying grid formation is made up of six-sided shapes.

Hue
This is a pure colour, without a tint, shade or tone.

Linoleum block
A flat piece of linoleum, which can be carved into a stamp and used in printmaking.

Monochromatic
This is a combination of shades, tints, tones and hues of only one colour.

Motif
This is an element or shape within a repeating pattern.

Non-directional pattern
A type of pattern repeat that is meant to be viewed in four directions. Motifs are

generally laid out in a geometric fashion in four directions so the pattern looks the same when rotated at 90°-turns. (See also Four-way patterns.)

Novelty print
A style of pattern where all or some of the motifs are recognisable objects. (Also called Conversational prints or Object prints.)

Object print
A style of pattern where all or some of the motifs are recognisable objects. (Also called Conversational prints or Novelty prints.)

Ogee repeat
A type of pattern layout similar to a diamond repeat, but with rounded sides to create a repeating onion-shaped grid.

One-way pattern
A type of pattern repeat that is meant to be viewed in only one direction. This type of repeat is common for novelty prints because of the recognisable nature of the motifs. (See also Directional patterns.)

Palette knife
A tool used for mixing paint or ink, which is available in a variety of shapes and is typically made of metal or plastic.

Pattern tile
A foundational, repeating rectangle or square that is the core structure beneath every repeating pattern.

Random repeat
A type of pattern where the motifs are scattered throughout the design and the repeat is not obvious or easy to pick out. (See also Tossed repeat.)

Repeat
This is a term that is used interchangeably with the word 'pattern'. (See also Print.)

Rosin paper
A thick, heavy-duty paper that is often used in building and construction, comes in large rolls, and is available at hardware stores. It makes a nice surface for hand-printed gift wrap.

Screen filler fluid
A thin fluid used in screen printing, which is painted onto the screen in order to block ink from printing through specific areas.

Screenprinting
A technique in which a design is transferred onto a mesh screen. Ink is then applied through the screen to print directly onto a surface like paper or fabric.

Shade
A type of colour created by mixing a colour with black.

Square repeat
A type of pattern repeat where the underlying structure of the repeating units is a grid-like formation. (See also Block repeat and Straight repeat.)

Straight repeat
A type of pattern repeat where the underlying structure of the repeating units is a grid-like formation. (See also Block repeat and Square repeat.)

Structured layout
A style of pattern repeat where the motifs repeat in a geometric, structured and predictable fashion. (See also Set layout.)

Tessellation
A type of pattern layout that is built on a foundation of interlacing and interlocking shapes without any gaps or overlaps. This type of layout is common in Islamic and Middle Eastern art and design.

Tint
A type of colour created by mixing a colour with white.

Tone
A type of colour created by mixing a colour with both white and black (grey).

Tossed repeat
A type of pattern where the motifs are scattered throughout the design, and the repeat is not obvious or easy to pick out. (See also Random repeat.)

Two-way pattern
A type of pattern repeat that is meant to be viewed in two directions. This type of repeat is common for novelty prints because of the recognisable nature of the motifs. (See also Directional pattern.)

Value
The lightness or darkness, also called the brightness, of a colour.

Watercolour paper
A type of thick, non-porous paper, often textured, and used in watercolour painting. It can also be used in drawing, painting, and printmaking applications.

CONTRIBUTOR INDEX

BLOGGERS AND DESIGNERS

Alessia Olivari
www.alessiaolivari.com

Ampersand Design Studio
www.ampersanddesignstudio.com

Anna Joyce
www.annajoycedesign.com

Barrington Blue
www.barringtonblue.com

BelloPop
www.bellopop.com

Hammerpress
www.hammerpress.net

Heather Moore, Skinny laMinx
www.skinnylaminx.com

Hitomi Kimura
www.hitomikimura.com

Jessica Swift
www.jessicaswift.com

Jonna Saarinen
www.jonnasaarinen.com

Karrie Kaneda, Happy Habitat
www.happyhabitat.net

Kate Sluman, Thrifted&Made
www.thriftedandmade.com

Katharine Watson
www.kwatson.com

Leah Duncan
www.leahduncan.com

Lisa Congdon
www.lisacongdon.com

Lucie Summers, Summersville
www.summersville.etsy.com

Mariam Eqbal
www.mariameqbal.com

Monaluna, Jennifer Moore
www.monaluna.com

MULK
www.mulk.co.uk

Pineapple bay studio
www.pineapplebaystudio.etsy.com

Rice Creative
www.rice-creative.com

Sarah Watts
www.wattsalot.com

Smooshi
www.smooshi.com.ar

Sophie Pépin
www.behance.net/sophiepepin

Susanne Firmenich, Hamburger Liebe
www.hamburgerliebe.com

The Soap & Paper Factory
www.soapandpaperfactory.com

Toodles Noodles
www.toodlesnoodles.com

Wit & Whistle
www.witandwhistle.com

Wolfum
www.wolfum.com

Zoe Ingram
www.zoeingram.com
www.lillarogers.com/zoe-ingram/

PHOTO CREDITS

Angel Tucker
www.angeltucker.com

Art Gallery Fabrics
www.artgalleryfabrics.com

Dan Rider
www.j6creative.com

Deana Levine
www.deanalevine.com

Eleanor at JEL
www.jelphoto.co.nz

EsteStudio
www.estestudio.com.ar

Jessica Nichols, Sweet Eventide Photography
www.sweeteventide.com

Lisa Warninger
www.lisawarninger.com

Ryan Gibson
www.shopchandra.com

Ryan Mason
www.ryanmasonimages.com

Scott Cormack
www.scottcormack.com

ADDITIONAL CREDITS

The collage mood boards on pp 16-17 contain images torn from the following magazines:
- National Geographic;
- Domino Magazine;
- Portland Monthly;
- and West Elm Catalog.

The flowers mood board on page 17 contains the following Creative Commons images:
- Poppy: Public domain image by Walkingbird96;
- Red and white paint: by Keely O'Shannessy.

Hammerpress gift wrap. Photo by Hammerpress.

INDEX

ACKNOWLEDGEMENTS

Thank you to my mum for instiling in me a strong creative spirit. I am forever grateful.

Thank you to my husband, Ryan, for believing in me all these years, even when I didn't always believe in myself, and for always standing by my side cheering me on.

Thank you to each and every contributor in this book. I am so honoured you all said yes to my emails and I am even more honoured at the privilege of sharing this printed space with your amazing talent!

Thank you to Isheeta, Erin and everyone at RotoVision, who worked hard to help me make a beautiful book and for believing in me enough to allow me to create it.

And so many thanks go to Jessica Nichols, the wonderful, sweet and talented photographer with whom I had the extreme pleasure of creating this book. It was an absolute joy working with you. Thank you for your friendship and for lending your talent to this book. It wouldn't be the same without you.

Jessica Swift

Jessica Swift rain boots. Photo by Deana Levine.